INVOLVEMENT ENGINEERING:
Engaging Employees in Quality and Productivity

Richard J. Pierce

ASQC Quality Press
American Society for Quality Control
310 West Wisconsin Avenue
Milwaukee, Wisconsin 53203

Published by
ASQC Quality Press
• Milwaukee •

INVOLVEMENT ENGINEERING:
Engaging Employees in Quality and Productivity

Richard J. Pierce

Portions of this book originally appeared
in the *Quality Motivation Handbook* by the
ASQC Quality Motivation Technical Committee,
copyright, 1967, American Society for
Quality Control. Reprinted by permission.

ISBN 0-87389-022-1

For Marie
My OAO, wife, and friend

ACKNOWLEDGMENTS

I wish to acknowledge the guidance, perspectives, and opportunities provided me by many people and many organizations that have prompted me to write this book.

The United States Navy appointed me Scientific Representative to the United Kingdom in 1951. That European post gave me my first opportunity to witness the increased productivity and quality that occurs without layers of management.

As a past Chairman of the Quality Motivation Technical Committee for the American Society for Quality Control, I received valuable information and input, which is reflected in this book. For this I owe my appreciation to the following committee members: Messrs. L. S. Dyrek, E. W. Ellis, H. Fritz, P. D. Metzler, J. A. Russell, H. E. Schock, Jr., S. C. Streep, and W. M. Weiss; Drs. D. A. Chambers, L. P. Sinotte, and F. B. Chaney; and USAF Col. A. B. Chelander.

I wish to acknowledge the excellent education in quality control I received at General Electric Corporation's Management Development Institute and the guidance I received from Quality Control Corporate Director, Dr. A. V. Feigenbaum, who approved my appointment as Quality Control Division Manager. I also enhanced my quality education through the assignment by GE Vice President O. Klima to investigate, adapt, and apply Japanese concepts and methods. From this opportunity came my first-hand experiences directing many quality improvement programs using steering arms, diagnostic teams, and my own applications of multiple-function quality circles and value analysis engineering teams.

Lawrence Miles, who gave birth to value analysis and engineering, taught me his discipline, which I was able to apply to my quality control and test operation, at General Electric. As a mentor, friend, and neighbor, he provided counsel on this book until his unfortunate death last year.

A proud occasion occurred when I was asked by Dr. J. M. Juran to write the "Quality Planning" section for the *Quality Control Handbook*. From writing this section, and particularly from meetings and correspondence with Dr. Juran, I gained an even stronger understanding of the role of quality control.

The George Washington University has provided me with many opportunities to share my quality philosophy by allowing me to organize and present symposia on the subject of employee motivation, management involvement, and the quality discipline.

Above all, I wish to acknowledge the help and support provided by my family: my son, Dick, Jr., and his wife, Jill, both authors themselves, provided counsel and guidance; and my son, Rob, besides providing input, acts as a vital link between management as I once practiced it and as he now lives it. The greatest help came from my wife, Marie, who reduced my draft manuscript from a tall stack of papers to a few pages of substance after her review. She also typed rewrite after rewrite after rewrite. And it was Marie's dinner parties — so I believe — and not my exhortations on technical subjects that enhanced my good relations with British officials.

Table of Contents:

New Basics:

- Development and application of manager's skills to improve environments, management style, and attitudes to enable more effective involvement and management of employees. (*See Chapters 3, 4, 5, and 6.*)

- Top official and upper management involvement and leadership. (*See Chapter 7.*)

- Ways to improve effectiveness of involvement of all levels of managers, professional employees, supervisors, and workers. (*See Chapters 8, 9, and 16.*)

- Revitalized attention to customers. (*See Chapter 10.*)

- Incorporation of quality and productivity considerations in strategic business plans. (*See Chapter 11.*)

- Continuous process of innovations, quality, and productivity improvements to products, services, and systems (*See Chapters 12 and 13.*)

- Effective company-wide and top-to-bottom education and training. (*See Chapters 14 and 15.*)

Figures:

Readings & Exercises:

CHAPTER 1
WHY AND HOW AMERICA LOST COMPETENCE WHILE JAPAN ACQUIRED COMPETENCE

WHY THIS BOOK?

This book tells managers how to apply the "new basics" developed by leading American corporations to compete with Japan and other nations. The "new basics" are the means by which these corporations improved their management style and quality and productivity, and demonstrated success in the international marketplace. IBM, Hewlett-Packard, Westinghouse, 3M, General Electric and AT&T are examples of these corporations.

The development of the "new basics" began when officials of these corporations learned why and how American industry lost its eminent international reputation for quality and productivity and why and how Japan acquired it. They gained insights about the key to Japan's success — namely, effective involvement and management of people, which is in contrast to America's emphasis on managing work. They saw the need to take advantage of improvements the Japanese made to the modern quality control discipline developed in America. They acquired appreciation of the effort required to adapt Japanese concepts for use by American workers. The ways by which American companies lost their reputation and the need for correction became obvious. But, it also became apparent that satisfactory response to these issues would yield only equality with Japanese companies. The leading corporations created additional innovations and improvements to attain superiority.

While different corporations use different terminology and emphasis, there exists similarity in the basic elements applied by these corporations to improve management style, quality and productivity. These elements are the "new basics." They form a road map by which other companies can achieve similar improvements. It is essential, however, that the managers of these companies learn, in reasonable depth, how America lost its reputation and how Japan replaced us. By understanding the role reversal, these managers will come to understand American industry's needs today and the importance of implementing the "new basics."

JAPAN'S CRITICAL NEEDS AFTER WORLD WAR II

After World War II, American Occupation Forces in Japan had first-hand opportunity to evaluate Japan's situation. It was bleak. With its immense population and small geography, there was insufficient agriculture to feed its people. Raw materials for conversion to products for their own use or for export were nonexistent. Early exports of toys and a few other products quickly created an international reputation for poor quality. There was no visible economy and no institutions to create it. There was a feeling of disaster.

1

The simple word "NEED" was the forcing function for Japan's successful effort to motivate its people, vitalize its economy and create its industrial revolution. This was the start of the competition.

America provided encouragement and support to Japan for developing its economy. Japan was not allowed to have a defense establishment. Hence, they could take resources which might have gone to defense and apply them to their economy. Dr. W. Edwards Deming's service was initially supplied by the American Occupation Forces. His contribution was a major factor in helping the Japanese achieve their success. Other consultants and forms of support were provided until the Occupation Forces were disestablished in 1952. Japan has had an uninterrupted opportunity, since World War II, to develop its economy and implement its industrial revolution.

Following World War II, America did not foresee the competition with Japan or with European countries. As the banker of our Marshall Plan, we were expending resources to finance the economic recovery of West Germany, Italy, France, Great Britain, Japan and others. Our resources were also going to support the Occupation Forces in Europe and Japan and to maintain the largest peacetime defense establishment in our history as required by the Cold War. The expense was greatly increased when America's economy was interrupted by the Korean War and Viet Nam War. The simultaneous funding of the "Great Society" and the Viet Nam War left less time and attention to our economy.

UNDERSTANDING AMERICAN MANAGEMENT'S LOSS OF COMPETENCE IN QUALITY

After World War II, American managers progressed from the "inspection" era of quality control to a modern, comprehensive discipline. This discipline begins in the marketing plans that introduce a new product; progresses through design reviews and acquisition from suppliers; involves control in manufacturing and assembly, including statistical controls; and is completed with final acceptance and customer use. This development was completed and the new discipline defined and published in the early 1950s. *Quality Control Handbook* by Dr. Joseph M. Juran, *Total Quality Control* by Dr. A.V. Feigenbaum, and *Engineering Statistics and Quality Control* by I.W. Burr are examples of the many publications released at that time.

Application of the new discipline swept the country and — as usual with something new — it was applied a little too enthusiastically. The new technique of "quality costs" initially revealed expenditures of 15% to 20% of a company's annual budget for prevention, inspection and control of quality, rework, scrap and response to customers' complaints. However, these costs eventually settled down to reasonable figures and American industry's reputation for quality control was unexcelled.

By the late '60s and '70s, however, the momentum had turned around. The economy had been affected by the Viet Nam War and the social programs of the Great Society. Quality became less important as part of a company's mission as new types of presidents and general managers took over "profit and loss" responsibility. The need to economize made "quality costs" a target when reducing nonproductive costs. Quality control personnel were the first to be put on layoff lists. Many scrambled to change careers. Industry had done a good job of educating and training quality control engineers, technicians, supervisors, inspectors and managers. But industry reduced its support, and education and training suffered. Suppliers shipped poorer quality material. Companies tolerated this and reworked it, passing the costs to consumers. Application of statistical controls decreased when it should have increased. The clout of the quality control manager had declined.

It is particularly important to understand that the application of quality control within a company has always been influenced most by the convictions of its CEO, president, or general manager. Individuals with high technology, marketing or finance backgrounds replaced the presidents, CEOs and general managers with manufacturing or engineering backgrounds. Their interests were different and their knowledge of quality and productivity less.

This is how American management lost its eminent position in quality control. It had the knowledge and a successful, debugged discipline with highly trained people. But it neglected to sustain and improve application.

UNDERSTANDING AMERICA'S NEGLECT
TO ACHIEVE MORE EFFECTIVE INVOLVEMENT

Following World War II, American management consultants and behavioral scientists became involved in research and development of ways to more effectively involve people in improving quality and productivity. Currently, articles and books describe an emerging industrial movement focused on more effective involvement of people. Actually the movement began in the 1920s and was accelerated after World War II. Publication of these concepts, theories and principles peaked in the '50s and '60s. While more effective involvement of people is the key to the success of the Japanese industrial revolution, American management failed to exploit the research and development of its own consultants and scientists.

Though American industry indicated respect, interest and support for some of the concepts, it applied greater effort to the "programs" approach for involving people more effectively. With little regard for the reservoir of research and development, American managers developed and applied such programs as "E" for Excellence, Zero Defects, Error Cause Removal, Pride, and Accent on Value. Despite the excess hoopla and exaggerated measurements, many excellent techniques for more effective involvement of people were created and proven successful. However, the benefits from the "programs" approach were usually of short duration.

3

Why didn't American management take the longer route to develop a foundation of understanding of the concepts, theories and principles of consultants and scientists? Why didn't they address the challenge and learn skills to create environments that could stimulate employees to improve quality and productivity? There are three answers: (1) There existed an unmanageable quantity of concepts, theories and principles published by over 200 recognized experts. (2) Most of these experts had difficulty leading the march across the bridge to application because they lacked knowledge and experience in the manager's real world. (3) America's priorities of technology and managing work were higher than managing people.

SELECTED AMERICAN CONCEPTS, THEORIES AND PRINCIPLES FOR MORE EFFECTIVE USE OF PEOPLE

The American Society for Quality Control (ASQC) was concerned that America's research and development was not being used. It sponsored a committee, the Quality Motivation Technical Committee, composed of leading industry and government managers, consultants and scientists. The committee was charged to review the works of all recognized experts and to visit and interview industry and government managers about application. The committee learned early in the game that only a few of the 200-plus experts had provided the most usable concepts, theories and principles. This was learned through intensive research of their work and from interviews with the users: i.e., managers. While 47 experts were selected for inclusion in the bibliography, the committee detailed the works of only nine in its final book, *Quality Motivation Workbook*, published by ASQC in 1978.

A separate investigation by the National Industrial Conference Board included a poll of 302 companies. While one or more companies recognized a total of 202 experts, only six were recognized by more than half of the companies. They were the same experts identified by the ASQC study. This book draws on selected experts, plus some Japanese concepts. Their work provides general indoctrination, measurements for determining "existing" environments, management characteristics, skills for creating environments, and management style.

LEADERSHIP FOR TRANSITION TO APPLICATION

An important insight learned by the committee is that skills and techniques for creating environments and motivating people must be the normal tools of a manager. Managers need to cross the bridge to learn the concepts, theories and principles of consultants and behavioral scientists and then return to lead the effort for application. Participation by other employees is better assured than when leadership is delegated to a consultant. There's a place for consultants. That place is to assist and teach.

When managers demonstrate the effort to become reasonably proficient in skills to involve people, and they provide the leadership for application, employees' support is strong and sustained. Where leadership is contracted to consultants or experts, employees' support quickly dwindles. This book assumes that skills for motivating people should be a normal part of a manager's competence and provides for his leadership.

When American companies first attempted to take advantage of Japanese methods, many failed because they tried only to copy the Japanese. Those who succeeded did so because their management took the time to study the philosophies and concepts behind the methods. Then they adapted these to methods suitable for American employees.

America's Failure to Adapt Successful Japanese Concepts

The Japanese studied America's modern quality control discipline and, quite logically, diagnosed some significant improvements. They also developed many original concepts. Initially, America failed to adapt these concepts because of false pride. Later, in some instances, it was presumed that knowledge of Japanese culture was a prerequisite to understanding Japanese business concepts. But, as Japan's products replaced American products, false pride and fear of an unknown culture disappeared. Thousands of companies have sent representatives to Japan. American and Japanese consultants are very busy teaching Japanese concepts. Despite this activity, only a relatively few American corporations have effectively adapted and successfully applied many worthy Japanese business concepts.

Most American companies could successfully adapt Japanese concepts. For example, the Japanese concepts of "Trust," "Subtlety," and "Intimacy," described later in this book, have their roots in Japanese culture. However, when a manager reads about them in a business context, he will note similarities with concepts by American experts, also described in this book. As the reader understands Dale Zand's "Cycle of Trust," Douglas McGregor's "Theory Y," and Rensis Likert's "Interaction-Influence Principles," he will also come to understand the above Japanese concepts and their applications. But he must recognize the difference between American and Japanese workers. He must carefully adapt the concept to American workers and not underestimate the training required. Other Japanese concepts, such as those related to company-wide quality control, relationships with suppliers, the "president's plan," quality circles, et cetera, are easier to understand. However the concepts cannot be copied. Effective training must be provided and carefully adapted.

Comparing Japanese Adaptation of Value Engineering with American Adaptation of Quality Circles

The concept of value analysis and engineering was created by Lawrence Miles, whose book of the same name was published in the '50s. It is a carefully developed, powerful technique for doing what the Japanese do best — continually improving the value, including the quality and productivity, of products. This is one of Dr. Deming's "14 Principles for American Managers." It is successfully applied in many American companies and continues in use.

5

Japanese management investigated and decided to adapt the concept for Japanese workers. Miles spent long periods of time in Japan teaching the concepts to Japanese managers. Groups of Japanese managers observed its application in American plants. They acquired extensive knowledge of the discipline and examples of its applications. Then they adapted the concept in ways that would be most usable by Japanese workers and engineers. Formal training programs were conducted. Miles made an annual trip to Japan, where he was honored and where he presented the "Miles' Prizes" to the companies and company divisions that had applied the technique most effectively.

The quality circles concept was developed by the Union of Japanese Scientists and Engineers (JUSE) to enable more effective use of their "*gemba*" or foremen. It was introduced in Japan in 1962, the same year Zero Defects was introduced in America. Hidesaburo Kurushima, former Chairman, Board of Directors for JUSE, dedicated publication of a series of brochures titled *Reports of QC Circles Activities* to Dr. J.M. Juran for his three lecture visits to Japan on quality and management and his interest in quality circles. By 1982, a New York Stock Exchange study reported quality circles in 44% of all American companies with more than 500 employees.

Dr. Edward E. Lawler III and Susan A. Mohrman conducted a study of the application of these quality circles in America. They reported that, to a large degree, quality circles have been a fad in America. In many cases, the CEO of a company had seen a TV program or read a magazine article praising circles and decided to give them a try. He or she then ordered the Personnel Department to start a few to see how they would work. In these cases, circles were simply something the top told the middle to do to the bottom.

Other companies sent teams to Japan, provided more serious preparation and achieved some successes. There is generally stark contrast, however, to the way Japanese management adapted value analysis and engineering and the way American management adapted quality circles.

UNDERSTANDING HOW THE JAPANESE
ACQUIRED COMPETENCE

The American Occupation Forces provided encouragement and assistance for developing the Japanese economy until the forces were disestablished in 1952. Eminent American consultants visited Japan in the '50s. Among them were Dr. W. Edwards Deming, an authority on management and a foremost expert on statistics. As a result of his major contributions, the Deming Prizes are awarded to the most productive Japanese companies each year. Dr. Joseph M. Juran is referred to as the Father of Quality Control in America. His three series of management lectures, his contributions in quality control, and his several books (translated to Japanese) were warmly received by Japanese management. Dr. A. V. Feigenbaum created Total Quality Control and taught it in Japan. Total Quality Control is the foundation of America's modern discipline. Lawrence Miles, the creator of value analysis and engineering, and founder and president of the Society of Value Analysis and Engineering, was widely accepted in Japan. As a result of his lectures and consultation, application of value analysis and engineering has become widespread in Japan. American corporations established in Japan after World War II provided major help.

The practice and application of the modern quality control discipline in America was at a high point during the '50s and '60s. The fruit was ripe and the Japanese harvested it with our help. During the '60s, hundreds of teams of Japanese managers, foremen, university professors, engineers and scientists visited thousands of American companies. They were routed by the American-sponsored Japanese Productivity Center in Washington, D.C., and Dr. Joji Arai, Director. They brought cameras and notebooks. The American companies presented seminars, gave tours and provided handouts. It was mostly all one way — because Americans had not recognized the existence of the serious competition. This activity by the Japanese also occurred in many other foreign countries.

To acquire competence, the Japanese had to sort and evaluate this information and then adapt the American concepts to methods suitable for Japanese workers. The task was immense. However, the Japanese enjoy closer relations between universities, professional associations, government organizations and industry. University professors, engineers and scientists from the universities and associations, along with government personnel provided competent assistance to Japanese management.

Concurrently, the Japanese recognized the power of education. They developed a high degree of competence in their educational systems. A larger percent of their young people graduate from high school than in America. Japan graduates more engineers than America. Their educational requirements, teacher competence, curriculum content and relationship to the needs of industry are superior to America's. In America, in the '50s and '60s, a student was challenged to pass the graduation requirements for high school. It was more difficult to gain admittance to nearly any college or university because of high academic standards. However, during the late '60s, the '70s and into the '80s, American educational requirements, curriculum content and teacher competence deteriorated. It was not until the '80s that actions were initiated to increase requirements and competence. In the meantime, Japan had a quarter of a century to produce better qualified graduates of high schools, colleges and universities to enter the job market for industry. The situation continues.

Japan's Key To Success — More Effective Involvement And Management Of People

While American managers spend much of their time on costs, schedules, and flow charts of work, the Japanese manager's first concern is the effective use of people to do work. This has been the key to Japan's success.

Many of their concepts are rooted in their culture. We have previously identified three central concepts governing their management of people. They are the triad of "trust, subtlety, and intimacy." A brief description will provide insights to Japan's primary strength. Detailed descriptions occur later in this book.

The concept of "trust" involves open communication, mutual trust between managers and workers, and the assumption that an individual wants to do his or her best. While much of the concept can be described by McGregor's "Theory Y" and Zand's "Cycle of Trust," its full meaning is best described by examples given later in this book.

"Subtlety" acknowledges the complexity of relations between people and the sensitivity and empathy needed to perceive them. This enables assignment of people who work best together to form the most effective teams. This freedom of assignment is given to Japanese managers and foremen without restriction.

"Intimacy," in Japan, is the caring, support and close relations between people — including managers, foremen and workers — that is applied both at work and outside of work. When economic and social life are integrated into a single whole, then relations between individuals become intimate. Values and beliefs become mutually compatible over a wide range of work and nonwork related issues. The relationship is "holistic."

Japan has demonstrated the importance of putting people first. America needs to do the same.

Japanese Management's Concept For A "Company Philosophy"

The Japanese believe the foundation of a company is its philosophy. Most Japanese companies operate from their company's philosophy but often do not formalize company objectives. American managers usually operate from their objectives, but do not formalize a company philosophy. Having a philosophy is like having a rudder on a boat. In America, the top official and his top management often struggle with difficult decisions. These may involve not only the welfare of the company, but also that of their workers, customers, suppliers, the community in which the company resides, nearby educational institutions, trade associations, and county, state and federal governments. Having a philosophy provides a compass to help guide decision making. Without a philosophy, there is no unity or coherence to decisions over a period of time. American companies would be richer, in a broad sense — and probably more profitable in the long run — if they developed company philosophies.

THE DOMINANT ISSUE OF THE COMPETITION

This book does not treat other issues of the competition between America and Japan. Frederick Richmond, an industrialist, four term member of Congress, and an authority on international trade relations, best expressed the reason when he stated that Department of Commerce records project it is obvious Japan will overtake the U.S. as the world's most productive economy during the '80s. While he describes other issues and means for competition which are being worked on or considered by the government, he emphasizes that they are all dependent on American industry recapturing the top position in quality and improving its position for productivity.

Other Existing And Emerging Competitors

West Germany, Italy, France, Brazil and Canada are examples of existing competitors who are replacing more products in America than we are replacing in their countries. The reason is the same — better quality products and higher productivity result in lower cost.

Additional perspectives on long-range American needs are gained by observing how the emerging economies of Korea and new initiatives from Taiwan are capturing major markets from several large Japanese companies. Initially the industries are shipbuilding, automobiles and some electronics. It is noteworthy that the Koreans created their new industries only after sending teams of managers to Ohio State University for a decade.

CHAPTER 2
NEEDS, APPROACH, AND OPPORTUNITY

WHAT THIS BOOK IS ABOUT

The purposes of this book are to inform managers how to involve all employees more effectively in improving quality and productivity and to reacquire America's national and international reputation as a leader in quality control.

To achieve these purposes, American management needs to regain the competence it lost and/or failed to acquire as described in the preceding chapter. But it is not sufficient to win the competition, nor to "return to what was" a logical challenge. We must improve on "what was" to sufficiently surpass the competitors. The improvements incorporated in this book come from:

- Acquiring and applying the management skills we failed to learn earlier to more effectively involve and motivate people. The skills should be developed from both selected American experts and from the Japanese.

- Taking advantage of improvements that Japanese management achieved in adapting and applying the quality control and management disciplines they acquired from us.

- Selecting promising characteristics that are unique to Japanese companies and adapting them for American companies.

- Gleaning the recommendations of Deming, Feigenbaum, Juran and Miles that tell American management what it must do.

- Drawing on successful adaptations of Japanese concepts and developments of new concepts by such innovative companies as Hewlett-Packard, IBM, 3M, AT&T, Westinghouse, Texas Instruments, General Electric and Corning Glass.

Finally, the needs of American managers to arrest the decline of American industry's reputation both at home and internationally and to regain its eminent position in quality control and productivity are comparable to Japan's needs after World War II. Both America's economic welfare and its national defense are at stake. The managers and workers of industry displayed their spirit and ingenuity in achieving the top position in quality control and productivity during the '50s and '60s. They showed their spirit and ingenuity by out-producing our adversaries in the two World Wars, and the Korean and Viet Nam Wars. Industrial competence was the primary reason for our success in these wars. Industry is the first line of defense. The current challenge draws on the same spirit and ingenuity of managers and workers of industry. They will find even more improvements.

NEEDS OF AMERICAN MANAGEMENT

The challenge is formidable. Our need to regain what we lost and incorporate the improvements is great. The overriding need is "how to do it," as presented below. American management needs to develop skills and acquire knowledge in:

11

- How to involve top management in creating a company philosophy and developing objectives for more effective involvement of employees to improve quality and productivity, achieve consensus and commitment, and establish a structure to lead implementation.

- How top, middle and front line managers can learn the concepts, theories and principles from a few selected behavioral scientists and management consultants and become familiar with the Japanese triad of trust, subtlety and intimacy. This knowledge provides the background of understanding that precedes development of management skills for creating environments and motivating more effective involvement of people.

- How to create a Management Workshop for developing the skills to create environments and motivate more effective involvement of people.

- How to develop a Supervisor's Training Program to improve the supervisor's role and increase the effectiveness of this vital "lynch-pin" between managers and workers.

- How to acquire knowledge of "existing" attitudes and the "existing" environment within the company, including gross misassignments of personnel, obstacles that prevent employee involvement, and opportunities for more effective involvement.

- How to develop criteria for a "desired" environment, correct misassignments, remove obstacles, exploit opportunities, adapt selected Japanese characteristics, apply incentives and change attitudes to attain the "desired" environment.

- How to acquire knowledge of customer measurements, judgments and competitive standing of the company's products, services and systems.

- How to acquire knowledge of measurements, judgments and competitive standings of the company's products, services and systems from other influential external American and foreign sources. This includes the corporate office, trade associations, consumer journals, competitors, suppliers, the community, stock analysts, *Standard & Poor's* and the *Thomas Registers,* and foreign sources.

- How to involve employees to tap into their knowledge of problems with products, services and systems and their ideas for improving quality and productivity.

- How to establish a continuing process for the improvement of the company's products, services and systems.

- How to identify the ways the Japanese have improved the quality control and management disciplines they acquired from us and adapt their improvements, where appropriate, to American application.

- How to achieve breakthrough to improve the quality and purchasing systems for the acquisition of suppliers, relationships with suppliers and means to assure quality of products shipped.

12

- How to achieve breakthrough to improve the quality system for inspection by application of more statistical controls and self-control and more effective assignment of quality control personnel, while reducing the numbers of inspectors, which will attain improved quality at lower cost.

- How to develop revitalized, comprehensive quality control education and training programs for quality control personnel, including courses to increase involvement of marketing, design, manufacturing and purchasing personnel who affect quality, and statistical control courses.

- How to make other improvements to personnel competence through education and training, relations with colleges and universities, and relations with professional societies.

We have provided a road map to summarize the above needs and the flow of work to achieve them, so the reader can easily visualize the total activity, select the best routes, and have a ready index to locate individual needs and solutions in this book.

The "New Basics"

The leading corporations organized the above individual needs into logical elements which I refer to as the "new basics." They recognized that the overriding "new basic" is *development and application of skills to improve environments, management style and attitudes to achieve more effective involvement and management of employees.* When credibility of management intent is perceived, then the other "new basics" can be introduced in appropriate sequence. They involve managers at all levels and provide them with means to effectively involve employees in improving the quality of products, services, and production systems while at the same time reducing costs.

When the "new basics" are applied by managers in this sequence, they become a system by which American companies can improve their management style, quality, productivity, and hence their competitive position. American managers will recognize many of the "new basics." But the challenge to American industry is "how to apply them," and that is the overall purpose of this book. The "new basics," in order of application, are:

- Development and application of manager's skills to improve environments, management style, and attitudes to enable more effective involvement and management of employees.

- Top officials' and upper managers' involvement and leadership.

- Incorporation of quality and productivity considerations in strategic business plans.

- Revitalized attention to customers.

13

- Ways to improve effectiveness of involvement of all levels of managers, professional employees, supervisors, and workers.

- Continuous process of innovations and quality and productivity improvements to products, services, and systems.

- Effective company-wide and top-to-bottom education and training.

APPROACH

Top managers must search for approaches that optimize opportunities for success and minimize risks. They are familiar with stories about the successful American companies and about those companies that tried but failed to adapt Japanese methods. The lessons learned from these experiences provide vital insights for achieving success.

Middle Managers

Middle managers have the most to gain by the changes described in this book. Their tendency, however, is to assume they have the most to lose. They've been paying dues on their turf for a long time so their initial reaction might naturally be to view change with suspicion and to proceed slowly.

Top management needs to demonstrate recognition for middle managers' concerns. The activities described in this book provide for their early involvement. Middle managers are informed of top management's intent to develop a philosophy and objectives and that they will have opportunities to contribute. They are invited, early, to participate in a program to acquire the background of American concepts, theories and principles along with the Japanese triad of trust, subtlety and intimacy. Many middle managers will be given key assignments to lead or participate in diagnostic teams and new quality circles for managers. They will assign their own representatives to "multifunctional" teams. They should be told that the changes will not change company organizations or reduce authority. The changes will help them to attain goals which are as beneficial to their careers as to their companies. They will acquire new skills necessary to their future careers and associated with the industry-wide movement for more effective involvement of people.

SEQUENCE AND ITERATIONS

While the sequence of the chapters indicates the order that activities are best implemented, there are a few key activities that require iterations.

The first example is the development of a company philosophy. It would appear desirable, at the beginning, to struggle through meetings to acquire consensus and commitment and finalize the philosophy. This would be the foundation for all future activities. However, the result should be labeled "preliminary." The knowledge acquired later about customer and other influential external sources, measurements and judgments, and after that, internal attitudes and environment, will affect the philosophy. There will probably be surprises, changes and additions. The same reasoning applies to development of objectives.

A second example is the development of "desired" criteria for the environment. Although the Management Workshop and the activities to learn "existing" attitudes and environment will be available for creating reasonably complete criteria, subsequent information will have an effect. That information includes problems and opportunities to improve products, services and systems, removing obstacles, use of incentives, and education and training opportunities. Evaluation of this information will result in additions and a few changes to the criteria for a "desired" environment.

The road map indicates the needs for iterations.

THE OPPORTUNITY IS NOW

There has never been a greater need to turn around the competition than now — and there has never been a greater opportunity to turn it around than now.

Since the beginning of the competition, after World War II, growth of the American economy was hindered by several factors: the need to share resources for the Marshall Plan, the Cold War, the Korean War, simultaneous funding for the Great Society and the Viet Nam War. Japan, West Germany, Italy, France and Canada did not have comparable disturbances.

After World War II, American industry made a respectable transition to peacetime industry, despite supporting Occupation Forces in Europe and Japan, banking the Marshall Plan to help other nations — who are now our successful competitors — rebuild their economies, and expending resources for the Cold War. It is important to remember that American management achieved a major breakthrough in quality control in a remarkably short time as it progressed from the "inspection era" to the modern discipline it has become. Dr. Juran published the first edition of the *Quality Control Handbook* and Dr. Feigenbaum published *Total Quality Control* in the early '50s. Before the decade was over, the new discipline had spread throughout American industry. By the mid '60s, however, a crossover occurred in the competition. Competitors' productivity rates exceeded ours. Consumers in America and foreign markets determined that our competitors' quality was superior to ours. In 1985 our trade deficits far exceeded any previous year and, for the first time, we became a debtor nation. There is a pressing need to turn the competition around now.

The American economy is more robust than it has been for several years. Hopefully, defense expenditures will not need to rise. National and state legislation is behind the recovery of our national educational system, which will provide more talented graduates for the job market. Universities and colleges who were not active in teaching the quality control discipline years ago are now eager to teach and take on expanded roles, as in Japan. Professional societies are equally as eager to provide increased support to industry in quality and productivity. All that is needed is better communication among industry, universities and professional societies. Significantly, there is an increasing interest in careers in quality control and productivity. And, of particular importance, there is an emerging movement throughout American industry towards more effective use of people to improve quality and productivity. This has been Japan's primary reason for success.

"New Basic" — Development and application of manager's skills to improve environments, management style, and attitudes to enable more effective involvement and management of employees.

CHAPTER 3
SELECTED AMERICAN AND JAPANESE CONCEPTS FOR DEVELOPING ENVIRONMENTS AND MOTIVATING EMPLOYEES

When the environment in which employees work is improved, then employees become motivated to improve the quality and productivity of products, services and systems.

The objective of this chapter is to identify the elements of a desirable environment, describe the criteria for these elements, and the characteristics to be avoided. Concepts, theories and principles of 17 selected American behavioral scientists and some concepts taken from Japanese sources are presented. They are the source of skills for managers to develop desirable environments and motivate employees — skills required of all managers. These skills will be taught in the next two chapters, the "Management Workshop" and "Supervisor's Training Program." We can accomplish this chapter's objective only if we take advantage of prior experience and lessons learned in unsuccessful attempts at attaining this objective.

Our forcing function is the reversal of the American and Japanese roles in quality and productivity. Japanese management succeeded by making more effective use of its employees. The Japanese concepts of trust, subtlety and intimacy enhanced the knowledge and skills the Japanese used to develop environments and motivate more effective use of people. In America's case, the words of William S. Rukeyser, a past managing editor of *Fortune* magazine, are appropriate: ". . . Many answers to quality and productivity problems have been ready to be plucked, like low hanging fruit, for decades." American behavioral scientists had developed concepts, theories and principles for developing environments and motivating employees to improve quality and productivity.

Initial concepts came from the Hawthorn Studies in the '20s, but the availability of concepts did not peak until the '50s and '60s. While many companies showed interest, this research and development was not converted to application, which was not carried out due to our belief in technology and major obstacles that industry faced.

The primary reason was the widespread belief that technology, rather than people, was the key to productivity and quality. Japanese management has demonstrated dramatically that attention to people must come before attention to technology.

It is important to note what the obstacles were, how they have been removed and the new means for involving employees. First was the unmanageable quantity of recognized experts — over 200 — who published a plethora of concepts, theories and principles. Second, concepts had changed as we progressed from the scientific management era, through the human relations movement, and into the behavioral science period — but human nature had not changed. The scientists who created the research and development couldn't cross the bridge to application because they lacked sufficient knowledge and experience in the manager's world. To many managers the concepts appeared as stark conclusions in a final scientific report. The words and format didn't relate to their use. There were no "handles." Managers were not acquainted with the term "behavioral science" or with the scientists.

A National Industrial Conference Board report contributed understanding of the term "behavioral science" through a list of common characteristics:

- It is an applied science.
- It is normative and value centered.
- It is humanistic and optimistic.
- It is oriented toward economic objectives.
- It is concerned with the total climate or milieu.
- It stresses the use of groups.
- It is aimed at participation.
- It is concerned with development of interpersonal competence.
- It views the organization as a total system.
- It is an ongoing process to manage change.

The American Society for Quality Control has been a leader in the movement for more effective involvement of people. Its national Technical Committee on Quality Motivation researched scientists and interviewed hundreds of managers, which resulted in reducing the quantity of experts from over 200 to the nine most favored by industry. This was quickly verified by a poll of 302 companies taken by the National Industrial Conference Board. While 202 experts were recognized by one or more companies, only six were recognized by over 50 companies. However, some new experts have since emerged.

The Society closely followed the progress in Japan. It presented the Society's coveted Shewhart Award to Dr. Deming for his work in Japan. The Society also observed American management taking short cuts to gain temporary benefits by creating motivational "programs" and "campaigns" with little consideration for the available research and development by behavioral scientists. The top managers in industry and government, who were the members of the Committee, interviewed and communicated with behavioral scientists. The Society, through its report to industry in the *Quality Motivation Workbook*, helped close the gap to application. The conclusions are as pertinent for American managers today as when published in 1967.

- The potential for improvement of product quality through improved quality motivation is very significant.

- The degree of this potential is much greater than stated in early literature or recent reviews.

- Enduring benefits in the area of motivation can be achieved through education on the concepts and the application of quality motivation as a *normal* management practice.

- Current literature generally agrees on the basic concepts for motivation. Many of these concepts anticipate extreme changes in general management practices; this evolution is not limited to quality management.

- While existing literature effectively documents motivation concepts, information on how to implement these concepts is at an innovative stage. The quality practitioner can contribute by learning to apply these concepts.

- The American Society for Quality Control will continue to review and develop information on quality motivation techniques and to distribute this information as a service.

- Full implementation of these concepts in industry and government is presently limited to a scattered few.

- The rate of implementation through management change may be a long-term process.

- The program or campaign approach is a tool of secondary value that may be employed effectively in many urgent motivation situations.

Today, obstacles have been removed, some mystique about behavioral science has been removed and new means for involving employees have been perfected. Top management can make commitments.

The road is clear, so take a brief look at the concepts, principles and theories gleaned from the 17 American experts and from Japanese sources.

WHO ARE THE SELECTED EXPERTS?

The 17 selected experts and their pertinent work are:

Chris Argyris	— Mix Model
Robert Blake and Jane Mouton	— Managerial Grid
Frederick Herzberg	— Motivators and Dissatisfiers
Charles Hughes	— Goal Setting
Joseph Juran	— Breakthrough Management
W. Edwards Deming	— 14 Principles for Management
Rensis Likert	— Interaction-Influence Principle
Abraham Maslow	— Hierarchy of Human Needs

Douglas McGregor	— Theory X and Theory Y
Lawrence Miles	— Value Analysis and Engineering
William Ouchi	— *Theory Z*
Richard Pascale and Anthony Athos	— *Art of Japanese Management*
Thomas Peters and Robert Waterman, Jr.	— *In Search of Excellence*
Dale Zand	— Cycle of Trust

If we review what each expert has to say, in sequence, we will learn they have much to say about many elements of the environment. We will note similarities in what they say although they say it in different ways. However, a craftsman cannot learn his trade by simultaneously learning to measure, plane, saw, chisel and hammer. He learns it one function at a time. You, in turn, cannot learn how to improve all elements of an environment at the same time. Unfortunately, some elements are so closely related they cannot be pulled apart. What helps is that the experts emphasize some sets of elements more than others. The approach taken below is to address sets of closely related elements.

The sets of elements and the experts associated with each set are:

Trust — Openness — Self-Control

Douglas McGregor	— Theory X and Y
Dale Zand	— Cycle of Trust
William Ouchi	— *Theory Z*
The Japanese Concept of Trust	

Management And Supervisory Characteristics

Rensis Likert	— Interaction-Influence Principle
Chris Argyris	— Mix Model
Robert Blake and Jane Mouton	— Managerial Grid
Thomas Peters and Robert Waterman, Jr.	— *In Search of Excellence*
The Japanese Concept of Subtlety	

Employee Needs — Goal Setting

Abraham Maslow	— Hierarchy of Needs
Frederick Herzberg	— Motivators and Dissatisfiers
Charles Hughes	— Goal Setting
The Japanese Concept of Intimacy	

Management Involvement

W. Edwards Deming   — 14 Principles of Management

Lawrence Miles   — Value Analysis and Engineering

American Adaptations of Japanese Quality Circles

Changing Attitudes — Achieving Concensus — Making Decisions — Implementing Change

Joseph Juran   — Breakthrough Management

Richard Pascale and
Anthony Athos   — *Art of Japanese Management*

For each set of elements we present the concepts, theories and principles of the selected experts. For Japanese concepts, examples are occasionally added to help explain the concept. A quotation from William Ouchi is pertinent:

> To a specialist in Japanese society and culture, the differences between Japan and the United States are so great that a borrowing of social organization between them seems impossible. To a student of *business organization,* however, the underlying similarities in tasks between Japanese and American businesses suggests that some form of the essential characteristics of Japanese companies must be transferable.

Ouchi and knowledgeable Japanese and American industrialists emphasize that many Japanese characteristics are worth acquiring but must be adapted to use by American workers, not simply copied. In this connection, John Hyatt, a businessman returning from Japan, made a vital observation: "We must account for the differences between Japanese and American workers in the acceptance of authority."

The selected concepts, principles and theories, organized in "sets," follow:

TRUST — OPENNESS — SELF-CONTROL

The ASQC Technical Committee on Quality Motivation and the poll conducted by the National Industrial Conference Board revealed that Douglas McGregor has influenced more companies than any other expert. His Theory Y remains the keystone in the construction of a desirable environment. The undesirable characteristics of Theory X, while not as prevalent today as when they first appeared in the '60s, do still exist and are to be avoided.

McGREGOR'S THEORY X AND THEORY Y

Theory X

Theory X describes the environment to be avoided. In today's world there still exist a few managers who have risen to the top quickly by application of Theory X. Mistakenly, they are given credit for being "hard-headed" managers who get things done in a hurry. In fact, the transfer or removal of such individuals has resulted in greater increase to productivity and attention to quality than any other actions to improve the environment. There are others in less responsible management and supervisory positions who can be identified easily and retrained. Beware of categorizing tough-minded managers under Theory X **unless** they have the characteristics of Theory X. They are often Theory Y advocates.

The undesirable environment for Theory X is:

- An environment of management vigilance over human beings who are assumed to be pious, permanently arrested in their own development and of limited individual initiative and ability, such as the factory "hand" of the past.

- An environment which keeps the implied threat of unemployment handy in case it is needed.

- An environment which does cater to security needs and obvious fringe benefits but is quite autocratic and possibly dogmatic.

This theory presumes that:

- The average human being has an inherent dislike of work and will avoid it if he can.

- Most people must be coerced, controlled, directed, or threatened with punishment to get them to put forth adequate effort toward the achievement of an organization's objectives.

- The average person prefers to be directed, wishes to avoid responsibility, has relatively little ambition, also wants security above all.

Why Theory X Fails To Motivate

The philosophy of management by direction and control does not motivate because the human needs on which it depends — the physiological and safety steps of the Maslow hierarchy shown on Figure 3.4, or the "dissatisfiers" identified by Frederick Herzberg, Figure 3.6 — are relatively unimportant in most industrial and government enterprises today. In fact, Theory X practices of authoritarian managers may have a negative effect, causing employees to behave in ways that thwart the objectives of the enterprise.

Operating under Theory X, the employee needs which are important, those centering on the social, ego and self-actualization steps of the hierarchy, are deliberately suppressed. The natural response of the employee is indolence, not all-out effort; passivity, not activity; compliance without real creativity; resistance to change, unwillingness to accept responsibility, and frequently unreasonable demands for economic benefits. As long as Theory X dominates the manager's thinking, the full potentials of average human beings are neither discovered nor utilized, and neither motivation nor quality motivation will be apparent except for occasional short-lived spurts.

Theory Y

Some of the criteria associated with Theory Y are:

- Theory Y is an invitation to innovation; any environment associated with Theory Y likewise requires innovation.

- It is an environment of trust, which changes by degree from a centralized management control and regulation of employees to one which permits greater *self-regulation*, and provides for an attitude of *helpfulness* rather than dominance, and *guidance* rather than control.

- It is an environment designed to get more out of people by allowing them greater freedom to voluntarily contribute more of their abilities to their tasks.

- It is an environment which associates company goals with the self-interest and growth of the employee.

- It is an environment which permits the organization to be propelled by employee motivation rather than using the organization to suppress that motivation.

The assumptions of Theory Y are:

- The expenditure of physical and mental effort in work is as natural as play or rest.

- External control and the threat of punishment are not the only means for bringing about effort toward organizational objectives. Man will exercise self-direction and self-control in the service of objectives to which he is committed.

- Commitment to objectives is a function of the rewards associated with their achievement. The most significant ego and self-actualization needs can be the result of effort directed toward organizational objectives.

- The average human being learns, under proper conditions, not only to accept but to seek responsibility.

- The capacity to exercise a relatively high degree of imagination, ingenuity, and creativity in the solution of organizational problems is widely, not narrowly, distributed throughout the population.

- Under the conditions of modern industrial life, the intellectual potentialities of the average human being are only partially utilized.

Why Theory Y Motivates

The implications of Theory Y management can be equated with the higher steps of the hierarchy of needs (Maslow). Theory Y provides a means to focus on dynamic conditions for motivation: it challenges the supervisor or manager to take full advantage of human growth and development, to provide for selective adaptation in place of a single, absolute control. Motivating people when Theory

Y is operating taps resources of substantial possibilities, instead of the least common denominator of the least skilled in the enterprise.

Further, under Theory Y, the limits of motivation are not the limits of human nature, but of the manager's ingenuity in bringing the higher steps of the hierarchy into play. In other words, if employees are lazy, uncreative and uncooperative, the potential of Theory Y is not being utilized by the manager. The latter really has allowed the dominant motivators to remain dormant.

OUCHI'S THEORY Z

Theory Z is based on the Japanese concepts of trust, subtlety, and intimacy. William Ouchi advises that Theory Z, quite simply, suggests that involved workers are the key to increased productivity. Further, he points out that the problems of productivity in the United States will not be solved with monetary policy nor through investment in research and development. It will only be remedied when we learn how to manage people in such a way that they can work together more effectively. And that involves trust.

ZAND'S CYCLE OF TRUST

Dr. Dale Zand of New York University states that the quality of motivation within an organization depends on whether its personnel are interrelated through cycles of trust or fragmented by cycles of mistrust.

Positive environmental elements are:

- Realistic communication and shared goals.

- Cooperative attitude between related organizational groups.

- Trust and openness.

- High quality-production goals established in part by employees.

Negative environmental elements are:

- Communication of minimum goals.

- Employee's standard is self-protection.

- Fear and hostility.

- Strong top-side control.

- Lack of confidence.

- Playing it "close to the chest."

Full development of the "cycle of trust" concept can result in favorable group interaction and goal sharing between groups. It appears that this concept facilitates transmission of company incentives into personal and group incentives at all levels.

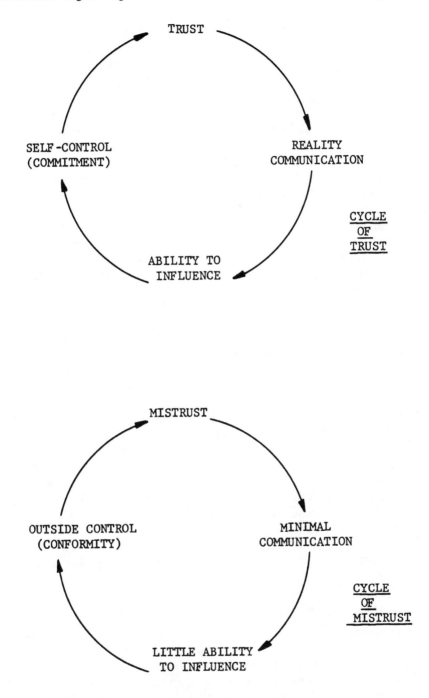

Figure 3.1 — The Cycles of Trust and Mistrust

JAPANESE CONCEPT OF TRUST

The Japanese concept of trust is reasonably similar to the American concept though the application in industry is more far-reaching. Egalitarianism is a central feature of Japanese companies and of Theory Z. Egalitarianism implies that each person can apply discretion and can work autonomously without close supervision because they are to be trusted. Trust underscores the belief that goals correspond, i.e., that neither person is out to harm the other. This feature, perhaps more than any other, accounts for the high levels of commitment, loyalty, and productivity in Japanese firms and in Type Z organizations.

It is noteworthy that McGregor's "Theory X and Theory Y" provide a connection between an egalitarian style of management and mutual trust. Theory Y advocates that motivation in work will be greatest when each worker pursues individual goals and experiences psychological growth and freedom. However, the style of supervision associated with Theory Y can be effective only when the supervisor trusts workers to use their discretion in a manner consistent with the goals of the organization, thus the connection of egalitarian management and mutual trust.

The following examples give insight about the more far-reaching applications of trust by the Japanese:

One example is related to several "profit and loss" centers within the same Japanese company. The nature of the business is that one center may have opportunity to profit at the expense of another center, and there is insufficient time for prior consultation. The success of the total company is dependent on such frequent transactions. Trust exists because it is known that such sacrifices will always be repaid in the future. Over time, equity is restored in the end.

Admission to an Imperial University almost automatically assures the candidate of entry into a major firm or government agency. University placement officials match students to employers on graduation. Both employer and students rely on these officials to make the best fit. Employers who fail to live up to promises of opportunity or developments are penalized in future years. Students cannot misrepresent their talents to an unsuspecting employer. To a large degree, the system is based on trust among employer, student and university official.

Lifetime employment in Japan applies to approximately a third of its employees. By extending this commitment, the employer relies on trust for the employee's loyalty to the firm and the employee's commitment to his job throughout his working years.

MANAGEMENT AND SUPERVISORY CHARACTERISTICS

Whether an environment motivates or demotivates employees is greatly dependent on the characteristics of managers and supervisors. The effectiveness of a company also is determined by the skills of its managers and supervisors in making individual job placements, and, of greater importance, in selecting individuals for teams. The concept that work equals talent plus motivation is often overlooked in determining personnel policies and procedures. Motivation, as well as talent, is an important factor in hiring, assigning, promoting, transferring and laying off employees. Positive employee motivation occurs within a company that has winning characteristics. A company with a reputation as a loser has demotivated employees. These environmental elements are interrelated, determined by management, and can be improved only by management.

Likert's "Interaction – Influence Principle"

Rensis Likert created finely separated characteristics of management, ranging from the unproductive to the most productive. They are collected into four systems of management, in order from least to most productive:

System 1 — Exploitative authoritative

System 2 — Benevolent authoritative

System 3 — Consultative

System 4 — Participative groups

Likert advises the above four systems and their accompanying organizational climates all exist in everyday practice. He contends that most of his attention is directed toward System 4 as it is the ideal for both profit-oriented and human-concerned organizations. He offers a large body of research to support his contentions.

Likert has a format for presentation of the characteristics that provides ready means for managers and supervisors to rate their subordinates, peers and superiors, as well as themselves. Subordinates can rate the manager and supervisor, too. (See Likert's Management Characteristics, Figure 5.2.)

Likert has also contributed the "Likert–type Scale." It is one of the most widely used scales in social research. The Management Workshop and the Supervisor's Training Program, described in subsequent chapters, make extensive use of the scale. They involve making a statement about an important issue, person or characteristic. Then, a person's reaction or opinion can be indicated by selecting one of several possible responses, ranging from extremes in both directions to neutral, or no reaction or opinion. (See Figure 5.1 for examples.)

Argyris' Mix Model

As a conceptual base for making change Argyris has developed the mix model. In the mix model he postulates six organizational variables, juxtaposed to illustrate the contrasting directions that psychological energy may take to determine the degree of psychological health or sickness. He calls these six dimensions "essential properties" of organizations. Dimensions that are diverted away from the essential properties are equated with further alienation of the individual and the organization; dimensions that are directed toward the essential properties are seen as buttressing the symbiosis of individual and organization objectives.

Mix Model

Away from the Essential Properties
1. One part controls the whole.
2. Awareness of plurality of parts.
3. Achieving objectives related to the parts.
4. Unable to influence its internally oriented core activities.
5. Unable to influence its externally oriented core activities.
6. Nature of core activities influenced by the present.

Toward the Essential Properties
1. The whole is created and controlled through the interrelationships of all parts.
2. Awareness of pattern of parts.
3. Achieving objectives related to the whole.
4. Able to influence internally oriented core "it" desires.
5. Able to influence externally oriented core activities "it" desires.
6. Nature of core activities influenced by past, present and future.

Figure 3.2

Clearly one issue at stake in the mix model is the source of power and influence in the organization. Whereas in the "away" dimensions power is central, in the "toward" dimensions there is an equalization of power and balance of power throughout the organization. In the "away" column, the first element — "one part controls the whole" — leads to the pyramidal concept of power centered at one spot, the top.

The "awareness of plurality of parts," element two, implies a view of a discrete unit of departments within an organization without seeing each unit's function in relation to the total effort. The third variable underscores this point in that each unit's objectives are self-serving, independent and narrow. The fourth characteristic implies rigidity and inflexibility on the part of the organism that makes it unable to change, modify and adapt its internal structure, roles, processes, or objectives to meet the demands of a constantly changing internal environment.

"Externally oriented core activities," the fifth characteristic, refers to the requirements of the outside environment, such as fluctuations in the economy or consumer buying trends. The sixth and final variable relates to a short-sighted approach to achieving objectives, maintaining the internal system and adapting for growth in the future.

Simply, the variables that are seen as aiding the organism to move toward the essential properties are polar extremes of the foregoing variables. In the positive or "toward" column, there is equalization and distribution of power and influence; there is an awareness of overall goals and objectives; there is cooperative effort expended in relating the unit's activities to the total objectives; there is an atmosphere of open communication and mutual understanding of functions and roles that permits internal flexibility and freedom; there is an attitude that welcomes change as a means of growth and advancement within the demands of the external environment; and, finally, there is a planned strategy of change, goal setting, and decision making, that takes into account past experiences, present demands, and the anticipated requirements of the future. Argyris is a proponent of group laboratory training. Such training is applied in the Management Workshop and the Supervisor's Training Program.

Blake And Mouton's Managerial Grid

The grid itself is a chart with two nine-point scales. On the left side of the chart is a vertical scale representing concern for people, numbered from bottom to top and from one to nine. At the base of the chart is a horizontal scale representing concern for production, also numbered from one to nine, left to right. On both scales number one is of low concern and number nine is of high concern.

Blake's Managerial Grid

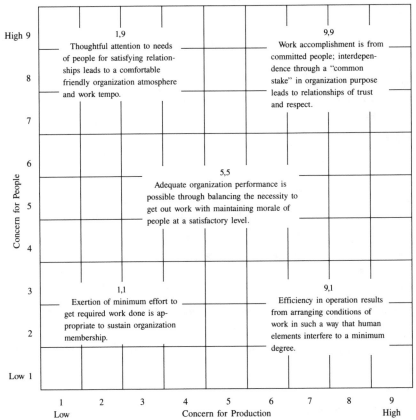

Figure 3.3

Theoretically there are 81 possible positions on the grid but it centers around five points or managerial styles:

9,1 is the caricature of the old-line autocrat with a maximum concern with production and an absolute minimum of concern for people. His conception of his job is to meet schedules, get production out, and tell people what to do. Blake calls the style "Task Management."

1,9 is the polar extreme of 9,1. The style is "country club management." The manager is concerned with a happy and harmonious work force, even though the company's need for products and services suffer.

1,1 is "impoverized management." The manager is not a leader. He has a minimum concern for production and for people. He simply doesn't manage.

5,5 is "middle-of-the-road management." The manager is moderately concerned for production and for people. He is a compromiser. In bureaucratic organizations, he often does well. But his real trademark is mediocrity.

9,9 is the "team management" style. It integrates a maximum concern for production with a maximum concern for people. The goal is development of 9,9 managers.

Peters, Waterman, And Company Characteristics

Experience has demonstrated that employees associated with successful companies are highly motivated while those associated with losers are demotivated. Thomas Peters and Robert Waterman, Jr. investigated 62 successful companies and reported eight basic characteristics that make them winners:

- **A bias for action** — a preference for doing something — anything — rather than sending a question through cycles and cycles of analyses and committee reports.

- **Staying close to the customer** — learning his preferences and catering to them.

- **Autonomy and entrepreneurship** — breaking the corporation into small companies and encouraging them to think independently and competitively.

- **Productivity through people** — creating in *all* employees the awareness that their best efforts are essential and that they will share in the rewards of the company's success.

- **Hands-on, value driven** — insisting that executives keep in touch with the firm's essential business.

- **Sticking to the knitting** — remaining with the business the company knows best.

- **Simple form, lean staff** — few administrative layers, few people at the upper levels.

- **Simultaneous loose-tight properties** — fostering a climate where there is dedication to the central values of the company combined with tolerance for all employees who accept those values.

There appear to be many clear relationships between the concepts, theories and principles described in this chapter. Their viability and creditability are verified by the winning characteristics.

The Japanese Concept Of Subtlety

When American dictionaries define "subtlety" we find such words as "tenuous," "intangible" and "obtuse." But we also find phrases like "mental acuteness or penetrativeness — the power or practice of drawing delicate distinctions" and "something that emanates from a subtle person as a fine drawn distinction, a refinement of analysis, perception or comprehension." A Japanese definition would connote an even deeper meaning and a closer association with the terms "intangible" and "obtuse." However, the Japanese practice of subtlety can be comprehended although developing the skills to practice it requires time and patience.

In Japan, subtlety deals with the complex relationships between people and the changes that occur within each person. The foreman who possesses it knows his employees well and what makes them tick. In enables him to optimize job placements, and, more important, he can put together work teams of maximum effectiveness.

The Japanese practice of subtlety no doubt encompasses many facets that appear tenuous, intangible and obtuse. Yet, American baseball managers possess just such mental acuteness and penetrativeness for making fine distinctions and perceptions when they form their most effective team, establish the most effective batting order and place players in the most effective defensive positions. The Chief Surgeon has it when he forms the most effective operating teams. The Head Nurse has it when assigning nurses for such duties as intensive care, the nursery, oncology and geriatrics. So do many American industrial managers.

However, subtlety is not something one learns in a "Management 201" course. It is a skill that comes from patient, long-term observation of one's employees, both their talents and their personalities. It involves human traits not apparent in tests for talent. There are few viable tests for motivation but the subtle manager will, almost instinctively, know what motivates each individual.

Obviously, the power or skill to practice subtlety is developed best in a participatory environment that permits close observations. Obviously it can only be practiced if turnover of personnel is low. Obviously the manager or supervisor must have complete freedom in the assignment of his personnel. Bureaucratic regulations or union contracts that prevent this freedom interfere with attempts to apply subtlety.

Subtlety is a management characteristic that can achieve substantial increases in productivity and quality. The reason it occurs is often obtuse and usually unidentifiable. While a primary application is in creating work teams, there are many other applications. Mental acuteness about happenings in the market place pays major dividends. A refinement in perceiving barely noticeable changes in customers' behavior and needs, or in competitor activities, can be exploited.

EMPLOYEE NEEDS — GOAL SETTING

Maslow's Hierarchy Of Human Needs

A long standing and still applicable concept about employee needs is Abraham Maslow's "Hierarchy of Human Needs." (See Figure 3.4 below.) Maslow's basic motivation theory concludes that:

- Motivated behavior is a channel through which *many basic needs* are expressed or satisfied simultaneously. An act typically has more than one motivation.

- Man is a perpetually wanting animal. His *needs* arrange themselves in a hierarchy. Every need is related to its current state of satisfaction or dissatisfaction.

- A want that is satisfied is no longer a want — *unsatisfied needs dominate motivation.*

- Motivation classification is based on *goals,* not on drives or motivated behavior.

- Motivation theory is not synonymous with behavior theory. In addition to motivation, behavior is biologically, culturally and situationally determined.

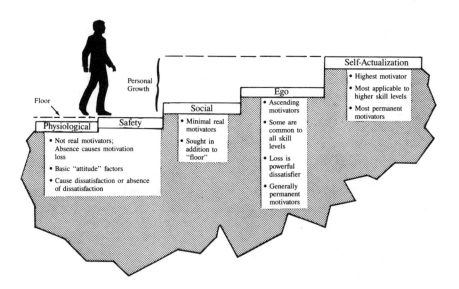

HIERARCHY OF HUMAN NEEDS & MOTIVATION

Figure 3.4

32

The Maslow motivation theory is expressed in a *hierarchy* of human needs. Programs and management efforts which provide for progressive satisfaction of human needs result in motivated action. Failure to meet a need which was once satisfied results in dissatisfaction and loss of motivation. The higher needs can only motivate if the lower needs are satisfied. Figure 3.4 illustrates the hierarchy concept and its relation to motivation. Note that the first two steps reach a "floor," or minimum needs. This figure includes some adaptation of Maslow's original terminology to relate to situations found in industry and government.

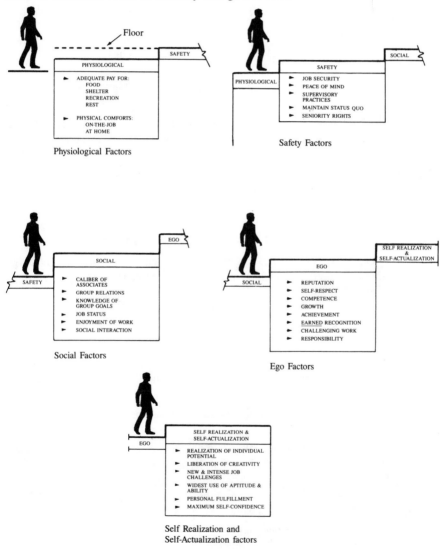

Physiological Factors

Safety Factors

Social Factors

Ego Factors

Self Realization and
Self-Actualization factors

Figure 3.5

Figure 3.5 translates the hierarchy of human needs into a set of typical work factors which impact "white collar" needs in almost any enterprise. Each of the factors illustrates one step of the hierarchy to facilitate understanding and discussion when this book is used by groups in training or seminar sessions. Depending on skill level and current state of satisfaction or dissatisfaction, various other elements can be utilized. Other elements can be drawn up to focus on the work factors for blue collar workers and specific groups.

Implications Of Hierarchy

Examination of Figures 3.4 and 3.5 leads to the conclusion that:

- Management attention should be focused on the higher needs.

- The higher needs will be ineffective if management fails to create the environment and conditions for the lower needs (below the floor).

- All of the needs, prerequisite for motivation and particularly QM, interface with several management processes.

Motivators And Dissatisfiers (Pittsburgh Studies)

Frederick Herzberg and his colleagues at the Psychological Service of Pittsburgh studied the work motivation of 200 engineers and accountants working for 11 Pittsburgh firms. Carefully controlled interviews were used to determine:

- Recent experience which made them feel particularly good or bad about their jobs.

- Effect of these incidents on their attitudes and on their job performance.

- Whether the impact was of long or short duration.

Herzberg concluded that the real motivators are factors which upgrade attitudes or performance; the other factors, which he called "hygienic factors" are prerequisites for effective motivation. They forestall serious dissatisfaction and make it possible for motivators to operate. When these (called "physiological" and "safety" in Maslow's hierarchy) were inadequate, they had a significant negative effect on attitudes, but they had no important effect when properly administered. However, when deprived of the "hygienic factors," motivation deteriorated very rapidly.

MOTIVATORS vs DISSATISFIERS (Herzberg)

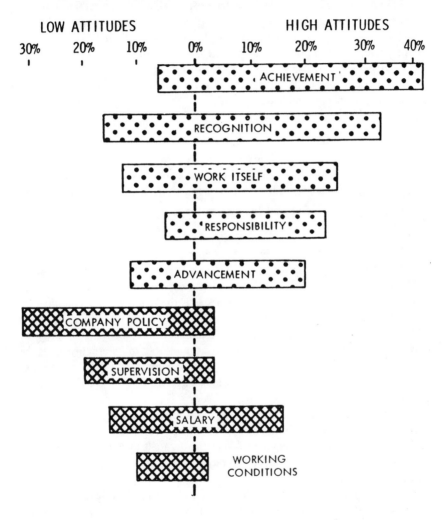

Figure 3.6

Figure 3.6 illustrates Herzberg's survey results in terms of the percentage frequency that principal motivators and dissatisfiers were mentioned.

An important conclusion, which is a fundamental behavior science principle, is that the effect of motivators and dissatisfiers is qualitative, rather than something measured in terms of sheer output. When people feel positive about their jobs, they put more *care, imagination,* and *craftsmanship* into their work; when they feel negative, they are not necessarily careless, but neither do they worry about fine details. In a word, favorable attitudes bring out their *creativity* and desire for *excellence,* while unfavorable attitudes dissipate their incentive to do more than comply with minimal requirements.

Hughes' Goal Setting

The prerequisite conditions necessary for successful synthesis of personal and organization goals can be stated as follows:

- An effective, understandable system for identifying company goals.
- A meaningful, clear system for setting personal goals.
- A system for achieving personal and company goal interaction.

Unless the company can determine where it is going, it will be impossible for its individual members to determine which direction they or the company are heading. Personal goal setting cannot work effectively unless the *company planning system* also works effectively. Performance review and personal development will have no point unless the company has established its objectives in a way which makes them just as understandable and communicable to its employees as they are to its top executives. True, company goals may exist. But they may be completely unyielding, cast into concrete which has hardened before they could be communicated.

This is unfortunate. Individual goal setting is futile where company plans have been made once and for all and cannot be changed. A person cannot be asked to find his proper place in a company, adjusting his goals to company goals, unless the company is willing to consider that modification of company objectives may, on occasion, be appropriate.

Neither extreme — communicable goals for all, or rigid, inflexible goals with no chance of change — is conducive to achievement, whether thinking in terms of the individual or the organization. This explains the importance of goal-setting systems specifically designed to produce involvement.

The derivation of company purpose involves human/organization purposes of the manager and other individuals. The organization's purpose is to serve society by facilitating the growth of the organization, its members, and its customers.

Hughes' summary of fundamental environmental elements include:

- An environment of trust which changes by degree from a centralized management control and regulation of employees to one which permits self-regulation.

- An environment to get more out of people by allowing them greater freedom to contribute voluntarily more of their abilities to their tasks.

- An environment which associates company goals with the self-interest and growth of the employee.

- An environment that provides an attitude of helpfulness rather than dominance and of guidance rather than control.

- Such conditions as freedom to speak, freedom to do what one wishes so long as no harm is done to others, freedom to express oneself, freedom to investigate and seek information, freedom to defend oneself, justice, fairness, honesty, orderliness in the group are examples of such preconditions for basic need satisfactions.

- Realistic communication and shared goals; increased informal communication, where appropriate.

- Cooperative attitude between related organizational groups.

- Trust and openness.

The Japanese Concept Of Intimacy

We have previously described the Japanese concepts of trust and subtlety. "Intimacy" is interrelated with them, but it emphasizes acquiring knowledge of people which includes individual employee needs.

In Japan, intimacy is involved with close relationships between people. It is concerned with the caring and support of the whole person. Since it is rooted in Japanese culture and history that far precedes its application in industry, we will only try to understand its application in industry.

Intimacy, in Japanese companies, is a concept that enables managers, superiors and subordinates to acquire knowledge about each other not only through business associations but through social associations as well. It is a holistic concern. Managers consider themselves obligated for social as well as business needs of employees. This detailed knowledge of employees and broad attention to their needs result in more effective management of employees. The understanding of managers' needs by employees assures more effective response to their direction.

In America, there is an understanding between employee and employer that the connection between them involves only those activities directly connected with doing work. The basis of this concept fosters objectivity and avoids emotionalism. At the same time, managers are frequently told they should maintain a sufficiently close relationship to employees because their performance can be affected by divorce, illness or death in the family, unusual debts, alcoholism, drugs, and other social events or conditions. American companies also sponsor baseball teams, annual picnics, cruises, hobby shops, dances, etc. American managers seldom go to such ends as the Japanese do to prepare dissemination of business concerns which are passed on to employees at these occasions, but they learn a great deal about each other.

In America, the solution appears to require a delicate balance between intimacy and objectivity. Some examples are given of Japanese applications of intimacy that can be adapted for application by American companies:

• Assign senior managers as counselors to college graduates recently hired by the company. Supervisors or senior hourly employees can also be assigned as counselors to newly hired hourly employees.

• Support symposiums by supervisors and hourly employees for supervisors and hourly employees, which are attended by managers.

• Support professional society activities and projects by making individuals and teams available. Initiate investigations on how to achieve more effective support by professional societies, as occurs in Japan.

• Support community social projects where benefits accrue to company personnel as well as community residents.

• Increase the scope of education and training within the company. Initiate investigations on how to achieve more effective support by universities and other educational institutions, as occurs in Japan.

MANAGEMENT INVOLVEMENT

Deming's 14 Principles For Quality, Productivity And Competitive Position

Dr. W. Edwards Deming is the internationally renowned consultant whose work led Japanese industry into new principles of management and revolutionized their quality and productivity. Dr. Deming's 14 Principles can also be considered goals for American management. They are obviously the responsibilities of top management.

The 14 Principles apply to small organizations as well as to large ones. The management of a service industry has the same obligations and the same problems as management in manufacturing.

The 14 Principles are:

1. Create constancy of purpose toward improvement of product and service, with a plan to become competitive and to stay in business. Decide to whom top management is responsible.

2. Adopt the new philosophy. We are in a new economic age. We can no longer live with commonly accepted levels of delays, mistakes, defective materials, and defective workmanship

3. Cease dependence on mass inspection. Require, instead, statistical evidence that quality is built in to eliminate need for inspection on a mass basis. Purchasing managers have a new job and must learn it.

4. End the practice of awarding business on the basis of price tag. Instead, depend on meaningful measures of quality, along with price. Eliminate suppliers who cannot qualify with statistical evidence of quality.

5. Find problems. It is management's job to work continually on the system (design, incoming materials, composition of material, maintenance, improvement of machine, training, supervision, retraining).

6. Institute modern methods of training on the job.

7. Institute modern methods of supervision of production workers. The responsibility of foremen must be changed from sheer numbers to quality. Improvement of quality will automatically improve productivity. Management must prepare to take immediate action on reports from foremen concerning barriers such as inherited defects, machines not maintained, poor tools, fuzzy operational definitions.

8. Drive out fear, so that everyone may work effectively for the company.

9. Break down barriers between departments. People in research, design, sales, and production must work as a team, to foresee problems of production that may be encountered with various materials and specifications.

10. Eliminate numerical goals, posters, and slogans for the work force, asking for new levels of productivity without providing methods.

11. Eliminate work standards that prescribe numerical quotas.

12. Remove barriers that stand between the hourly worker and his right to pride of workmanship.

13. Institute a vigorous program of education and retraining.

14. Create a structure in top management that will push every day on the above 13 points.

Miles' Value Analysis And Engineering

Value analysis and engineering (VAE) is an American invention. It was created by Lawrence D. Miles while he was an employee of the General Electric Corporation. The first edition of Miles' book was published in the '50s and application gradually spread throughout industry. The Japanese were quick to recognize that the system is a unique and effective tool to improve quality and productivity. It spread rapidly in Japan. The Japanese created the Miles Award which is presented to Japanese companies and divisions of companies each year for accomplishments achieved through the use of VAE. Each year Miles was requested to come to Japan to present the awards. There is currently a major resurgence in the use of VAE in the United States and several other countries.

The VAE concept is based on the consideration that all costs relate to functions and there may be alternate ways to accomplish the function that will achieve greater value. The system has three basic steps:

1. Identify the function.

2. Evaluate the function by comparison.

3. Develop value alternatives.

Value analysis and engineering is oriented to solving many categories of problems. These include management decision-type problems, product problems and service problems.

Special knowledge and procedures are required so training is a prerequisite. The system is normally applied through specially formed value analysis and engineering teams. Much care is taken in the selection of the team, which must be tailored to the identified problems. In many cases, the problems require considerable involvement of professional personnel.

AMERICAN ADAPTATIONS OF JAPANESE QUALITY CIRCLES

Quality Circles — The Original Concept

The start of the QC circles in Japan is generally attributed to a project begun in 1961 by the editors of the Japanese magazine, *Quality Control,* which sponsored a symposium in one issue on "Some Problems Facing the Shop Foremen." From this symposium two ideas emerged. First, there was need for a quality control magazine which was more "down to earth" — closer to the shop floor — than existing publications. Second, there existed a lack of opportunities for foremen to air their opinions outside the factory. The editorial board of *Quality Control* thereupon set up a discussion session on "The Duties of the Shop Foreman in Quality Maintenance" as part of the Annual Quality Control Conference held in November, 1961, and invited shop foremen to join the panel.

The next step was the editors' sponsorship of *The Foreman and QC (Gemba to QC),* a magazine for shop people, first published in July, 1962. Initially published quarterly, it has since become a monthly journal. It was designed to promote education and training at the first level of shop supervision, and its price was set low enough to make it attractive to first level supervisors and workers who would have to buy it with their own money. In addition to sponsoring the new magazine, the editors decided to sponsor the organization of QC Circles, to be led by supervisors or working foremen which could become the nucleus of quality control activities within a plant.

Quality Circles — Unsatisfactory American Applications

Quality circles expanded rapidly in Japan. The three circles created in 1962 grew to 40 before year-end. Within approximately five years there were 16,000 circles with 200,000 members.

It took a while before quality circles traveled to America. By 1982, 44% of all American companies with over 500 employees had quality circle programs and 75% of those started after 1980. Over 90% of the Fortune 500 companies now have quality circle programs.

In some cases, quality circles were adapted and applied wisely with good results. But in many cases, American companies went to consulting firms for training and the result was simply copies of Japanese programs. Cultism and buzz words were prevalent. Dr. Edward Lawler and Susan Mohrman studied implementation in a significant number of American companies and reported their results early in 1985. They concluded, "Although quality circles provide real benefits for both management and employees, they have significant limitations. They have also tended to be self-destructive." The phases of implementation and associated reasons for destruction are indicated in Figure 3.7.

Phases of a circle's life		
Phase	**Activity**	**Destructive forces**
Start-up	Publicize	Low volunteer rate
	Obtain funds and volunteers	Inadequate funding
	Train	Inability to learn group-process and problem-solving skills
Initial problem solving	Identify and solve problems	Disagreement on problems
		Lack of knowledge of operations
Approval of initial suggestions	Present and have initial suggestions accepted	Resistance by staff groups and middle management
		Poor presentation and suggestions because of limited knowledge
Implementation	Relevant groups act on suggestions	Prohibitive costs
		Resistance by groups that must implement
Expansion of problem solving	Form new groups	Member-nonmember conflict
	Old groups continue	Raised aspirations
		Lack of problems
		Expense of parallel organization
		Savings not realized
		Rewards wanted
Decline	Fewer groups meet	Cynicism about program
		Burnout

Figure 3.7

New Concepts For Quality Circles

Guidance for successful Americanized adaptations for quality circles comes from this investigation and other successful experiences by American companies. This includes managers' quality circles as well as supervisor/hourly employees' quality circles. Examples are:

- Use quality circles for *Special Projects*. The external and internal diagnostic teams described in Chapter 7, are examples of managers' quality circles. Both managers' quality circles and supervisor/hourly employees' quality circles are excellent means for forming multifunctional teams to support diagnostic teams. Initially, they identify problems and opportunities for improvement. Later they become involved in goal setting and planning as well as implementing improvements within their competence.

- Use quality circles as a *Transition Vehicle*. When setting goals and developing plans, a circle sometimes reaches its limit technically. The circle has served an excellent function by identifying the problem and potential opportunity. The task can then be turned over to that part of the organization with the technical competence, or to a value analysis and engineering team that includes the necessary technical people.

- Use quality circles to *investigate and improve systems of production or systems for providing services*. Quality systems breakthrough teams are an example. Such teams include senior managers and professional personnel from several organizations. They deal with professional problems associated with quality control, material procurement, and production more than with electronics, hydraulics, and other engineering disciplines.

The company must rely more on its own personnel to determine what quality circles are to be used for and how to adapt the concept to American personnel. They should be more concerned with the training program and they must lead implementation. Consultants can help teach and provide counsel. Some American companies have used personnel department specialists as instructors and facilitators. In these cases, employees usually do not sustain interest. If the company's work is engineering, use engineers. If it is accounting, use accountants. Both the Management Workshop and the Supervisor's Training Program include training for quality circles.

Quality circles should not be started or approved and then set adrift with the expectation that they will continuously identify new problems and innovate new solutions. They should be assigned or approved by a designated authority. They should be given guidance about the goals, and supplied with funds or other resources as needed and authorized. The president's plan, also described in Chapter 7, is an example of a vehicle that provides authority and releases resources if needed. The circle should be given opportunity to describe its progress to superiors and peers. Continued implementation, redirection, suspension or cancellation should be made as appropriate.

The concept of a magazine or paper for supervisors and hourly employees, which includes contributions from them, is a good one. So is the concept that permits symposiums and seminars for supervisors and hourly employees.

CHANGING ATTITUDES — ACHIEVING CONSENSUS — MAKING DECISIONS — IMPLEMENTING CHANGE

The new movement throughout industry for more effective use of people to improve quality and productivity requires major changes in management style and greater emphasis on long range planning. Dr. Joseph Juran has developed a concept of breakthrough management, sponsored by the American Management Association, that is particularly applicable to our needs.

Juran's Breakthrough Management

The successful companies have learned from the experience of those who have failed. A common reason for failure is underestimating the effort required to change attitudes along with lack of an orderly approach to implementing the change. Breakthrough management addresses the problem of changing attitudes and provides carefully planned steps of "unvarying sequence" that offer guidance in changing attitudes and effecting major changes.

First, Dr. Juran contrasts control and breakthrough. Control means staying on course, adherence to standard, and prevention of change. Breakthrough means change, a dynamic, decisive movement to new and higher levels of performance. Additional contrasts are given in Figure 3.8.

Sequence of Events	For Control	For Breakthrough
The facts needed are usually	Simple, showing actual performance vs. standard performance.	Complex, to permit deeper understanding of the problem than ever before.
The facts are usually collected by	"Regular" scorekeepers, i.e., accountants, inspectors, etc.	A special fact-collecting team, i.e., task force, staff specialist, etc.
Formality of fact collection is usually	Absent. Often there are not even permanent records.	Present. May require special experiments, tests, and formal reports.
The facts are usually analyzed by	The "line" people, i.e., foreman, branch manager or, frequently, nonsupervisory personnel.	Technical people or specially trained analysts.
Frequency of analysis is usually	High. May require monthly, weekly, daily, or hourly review.	Low. Often is only a one-shot analysis.
Decision for action is usually by	The "line" people responsible for meeting the standard.	Upper-level supervision, since interdepartment changes are involved.
Action is usually taken by	The "line" people responsible for meeting the standard.	Departments other than those responsible for meeting the standards.

Figure 3.8

The concept applies an unvarying sequence by which we break out of old levels of performance and into new.

The starting point is the attitude that a breakthrough is both desirable and feasible. In human organizations, there is no change unless there is first an advocate of change. If someone does want a change, there is still a long, hard road before change is achieved.

The second need is to see whether a breakthrough is likely to happen if we mobilize for it — a sort of feasibility study. In most situations, this feasibility study includes an analysis to separate the major parts of a problem from the rest — separating the "vital few" from the "trivial many." Dr. Juran calls this Pareto Analysis. Pareto Analysis is a management tool of uncommon power and versatility. It finds the few needles of vital problems in a haystack of trivia. These vital few problems then become the subject of a drive for new knowledge.

Organization for breakthrough in knowledge is next. It requires that we appoint or create two pieces of organizational machinery. One is for directing the breakthrough in knowledge, the other for doing the fact gathering and analysis. We will call them the Steering Arm and the Diagnostic Arm, respectively. The Steering Arm has the job of directing the acquisition and use of the new knowledge. But new knowledge requires research, which in turn requires direction, facilities and theories. The Diagnostic Arm does the detailed work of fact collection and analysis needed to achieve the breakthrough in new knowledge and to pave the way for action.

Breakthrough in the cultural pattern is, in this way, an added essential step. Before the new levels of performance can be reached, we must discover the effects of the proposed changes on the cultural pattern, and find ways to deal with the resistances generated.

Breakthrough in performance can now be achieved.

Control, during and after attainment of the new level, becomes the final step.

The reader will note the application of Juran's Breakthrough Management in this book.

Pascale And Athos On The Japanese Approach For Achieving Consensus And Making Decisions

Richard Pascale and Anthony Athos describe a Japanese approach for achieving consensus and making decisions. The Japanese recognize, as much as we do, that decisions must be made. However, when they have the time, they prefer to invest it in carefully building a foundation of support. They recognize that many more elements of an organization will be strongly committed to a decision if they take part in it. The Japanese feel that not only do consultative decisions result in better decisions but that it is their *obligation* to include other people.

A Japanese manager will plan the steps of the decision-making process carefully. He will make sure all parties affected by the decision, and particularly those who must implement it, are thoroughly briefed. They will be given opportunity for discussion and involvement. The decision is reached after all options and opinions are considered and after all details have been explored. In fact, consensus is developed before the decision is finalized. When formalized, the decision is expressed in depth and in detail that assures no loose ends. Implementation is assured as the implementors were part of the process. Cooperation by affected parties is assured because all their concerns were considered.

"New Basic" — Development and application of manager's skills to improve environments, management style, and attitudes to enable more effective involvement and management of employees.

CHAPTER 4
THE MANAGEMENT WORKSHOP

INTRODUCTION

The ultimate objective of the Management Workshop is to provide the skills and techniques for making more effective use of employees to improve quality and productivity. It is important to keep the ultimate objective in mind so we don't flounder along the way with an obsession for sensitivity training, perfection of techniques, or procrastination on applications to improve products, services and systems.

Realization of the ultimate objective is based on an axiom of behavioral science. Improvement in the employees' working environment, and balanced rewards to employees as well as to the company, induce employees to become self-motivated in improving quality and productivity. The process can be explained by analogy with a table. Behavioral scientists have identified the environmental elements that motivate employees and the rewards that provide greatest satisfaction. These elements and rewards are the legs to a table that supports a mass of quality and productivity. If "existing" conditions for the elements and "existing" rewards fail to meet the criteria provided by the scientists, the legs are weak and the table can support only a light load of quality and productivity. As existing conditions and rewards are changed toward the criteria, the legs become stronger and the table will support a heavy load of quality and productivity.

The development of most behavioral science concepts, theories and principles occurred in the '60s and earlier. Those used in the workshop were selected by managers of industry through interviews and polls. They have been reinforced and built on by other eminent scientists. The greatest concepts, theories and principles are too important to be new. Few major concepts have been created since the '60s. However, innovative adaptations have occurred and, of course, Japanese concepts have received much attention. The workshop uses the new adaptations and several Japanese concepts.

USE

This book recognizes that improving or maintaining competitive position is a vital and never ending concern of top management. It has become common to be "blind sided" by a competitor. Constant vigilance is necessary. Therefore, the structure and the process for attaining improvements to products, services and systems are of a continuous nature.

The Management Workshop will include numerous exercises to develop skills for more effectively involving people. These exercises will not be related to fictitious situations but will be based on actual situations which may occur in your company and will generate solutions for dealing with them.

Top management is usually constrained by conventional organizations that, for example, put all design engineers in one group, all manufacturing types in another, the purchasing agents in yet another and the quality control specialists in their separate organization. Organizational boundary lines of high tensile strength keep these groups separated. Yet, most issues and problems within a company require the contributions of individuals from several disciplines who work as a team. The steering arm, diagnostic and support teams described in the book are examples in which membership is from several different organizations or disciplines.

APPROACH TO TEACHING

An individual reader can substantially improve his knowledge, skills and techniques by self-teaching. His perspective and talent will be enlarged if the individual participates in a group such as a workshop sponsored by his company or even a self-initiated group. For the most part, the approach to teaching involves five steps:

1. To acquire knowledge about a concept or technique from available material. The material comes from the selected concepts, theories, and principles described in Chapter 3 and is augmented by additional material in this chapter.

2. To acquire initial skills through execution of written exercises that apply the above knowledge to the conditions or the people at the manager's company.

3. To expand and reinforce skills through group discussions and interactions. Managers learn by observing and analyzing other managers' interpretations and applications of the knowledge.

4. To review and revise the exercises, based on the group discussions and interactions, to provide a guide for application at the manager's company. These guides become the manager's personal workbook.

5. To follow-up by reviewing the manager's on-the-job strengths and weaknesses in application and to prescribe means to correct weaknesses.

INSTRUCTORS

While the initial objective is to teach the concepts of the behavioral scientists, the ultimate objective is application of the concepts to achieve improved quality and productivity. Instructors who are both expert in the science of human behavior and experienced in the manager's world are difficult to find. Experience has demonstrated a workshop is more apt to flounder if instructors are behavioral scientists with only experience in *observation* of the manager's world. They are more proficient in meeting the initial objective but frequently falter in attaining the ultimate objective. The more successful workshops are those whose instructors have had extensive management experience and have been given opportunity to acquire knowledge of the more vital concepts, theories and principles of the scientists. They seldom lose sight of the ultimate objective and are more proficient in removing obstacles, exploiting opportunities and making more effective use of people in disciplines they are familiar with — quality and productivity.

The best option for top management is to select one or two individuals who have had a wide scope of experience in management, who have exhibited skill in interpersonal skills on the job, and who are respected within the company, and to designate them as the instructors. The top official, or the steering arm, should explain what is expected of the instructors and should provide an overview of their activities. The preceding chapter, "Selected American and Japanese Concepts for Developing Environments and Motivating Employees," provides a good starting place for the instructors. Further knowledge can be gained by utilizing sources listed in the bibliography, by attending university workshops and professional seminars, and by networking with instructors in other companies.

An optimum class size for one instructor is 20. The group of 20 is broken down to subgroups of four or five individuals. The minimum duration of a class is one week of full-time sessions plus short duration follow-up sessions. For most companies, it requires several months before all managers can be processed through the workshop.

ATTENDEES

All managers in a company are involved with productivity and most have an impact on quality of products or services. The workshop is for all managers of all organizations. While there is an overriding sequence for scheduling attendees, i.e., from top management downwards, the workshop provides opportunities for different echelons of management to understand each other's problems better. Thus, some mixture of management levels in each class is desirable.

The workshop also provides opportunities to reduce adversarial relationships between two organizations. For example, production control managers, who push schedules, and quality control managers, who stress quality, are often adversaries. A similar condition often exists between purchasing managers and quality control managers. By mixing such managers in the same class, barriers between organizations can be lowered.

SEQUENCE

First, the workshop addresses the three basics: empathy, self-esteem, and rewards. Then individual elements of the environment are addressed.

Empathy is the understanding of another person's feelings and motives. It is the ability to identify oneself with another person so as to understand their point of view and what influences them. Empathy is the key to practically all the work of teachers, preachers, psychiatrists, parents and others whose vocation depends on the influencing of people. A manager's career is dependent on his ability to influence superiors, peers and subordinates including influencing improvements to environments, quality and productivity.

Self-esteem is self-respect. It is esteem for oneself and esteem by others. It is the regard we have for our own standing or position in life. A manager must realize that the self-esteem of individual employees is the underlying goal as he develops improved environments, provides rewards and motivates performance.

Then come *rewards.* Most behavioral scientists have dealt with the vital need for rewards. The most effective rewards are tied to certain types of employee needs. The trend is for companies to balance benefits for the employees with benefits to the company. Employees are sensitive to a situation where they are asked to make a commitment to more effective involvement which increases the company's business and profits — they then believe they deserve a share. It is noteworthy that, as unions are losing clout for winning benefits for employees, federal and state governments are introducing legislation that results in new benefits or protection of existing benefits. Rewards are essential to achieving more effective use of employees.

Following the three "basics" — empathy, self-esteem, and rewards — the elements for improving environments, management style, and attitudes are addressed in Chapter 5.

PART I. EMPATHY

CONTENTS:

Reading   — What is the Other Person's Point of View?

Exercises — Placing Yourself in Your Employees' Shoes

Relationship Analyzer and Planner

Activity A. Descriptive Analysis

Activity B. Contribution Analysis

Activity C. Improvements

READING — WHAT IS THE OTHER PERSON'S POINT OF VIEW?

Empathy is the process of grasping or understanding the other person's point of view — putting yourself in his shoes or viewing a situation or idea through his "filter." It can be one of the most valuable, powerful characteristics you can develop to strengthen interpersonal relations, communications and the ability to get things done through people.

Everyone but a hermit practices empathy to some degree, but most of us can very profitably extend its use to other areas of our lives and make it an increasingly automatic habit.

Empathy does not involve *acceptance* of the other person's viewpoint, but the development of an increasingly clear *understanding* of the way that person is serving the situation. In some cases it may be intermixed with sympathy, the acceptance of the other person's idea or *feeling* the way he feels, but these are two distinctly different processes. Either may be observed in isolation, or they may be (and usually are to some degree) in action simultaneously.

There are three definite steps in the practice of empathy. As it becomes a more automatic habit the three steps flow in a smooth, fluid sequence, but it helps to recognize and understand each stage. Here they are:

1. Recognize that every person in the world has his own personal, unique, individual filter through which he perceives reality. It is made up of education, childhood training, attitudes, prejudices and countless experiences.

2. Accept this fact as a good system. Be willing to allow the other person the right to be himself and to see reality in his own way. This doesn't mean you should necessarily *like* the other person's point of view — just that you do not insist that everyone think exactly as you do.

3. Only to the degree that the first two steps have been taken can one proceed to crawl into another's filter and see how the world looks from in there. Of course, this can never be done perfectly because we can never completely set aside our own point of view. But the entire process of communication between human beings can certainly be strengthened and enriched to the degree that those communicating do grasp or understand the various elements of the filter mechanisms with which they are dealing.

Try these three steps in your relationships with your employer or employee — your spouse — your children or parents — people of other religious or political persuasions. You will find that as empathy becomes a habit your ability to relate effectively with people, to motivate them and to achieve your goals in life will be multiplied manyfold.

EXERCISE — PLACING YOURSELF IN YOUR EMPLOYEES' SHOES

Purpose

- To help you place yourself in your employees' "shoes" and to better understand their feelings and points of view.

- To help you identify the differences between your employees.

Procedures

Individual Work

- Assume you are one of your employees (Employee A) for the next few minutes.

- Take about five minutes to complete the questionnaire, "My Manager's Style," as you think this employee would complete it.

- Next do the same with Employee B.

- Do this also for Employee C.

(Time: 15 minutes)

51

Group Work

• In your small group, share with each other the things you have learned as a result of this exercise.

• List on chart paper the major ideas, insights, etc., discussed and be prepared to report these to main workshop group.

(Time: 25 minutes)

"My Manager's Style"

Statements below, arranged in pairs, represent supervisory style. Assign a weight from 0 to 10 to each statement to show the relative accuracy of the statements in each pair for describing your supervisor's style. The points assigned for each pair must in each case total 10.

1 —Easy to talk to, even when under pressure.   _____

—You have to pick carefully the time when you talk
to him.   _____
                                                                       10

2 —May ask for ideas, but usually his or her mind is
already made up.   _____

—Tries to see the merit in your ideas even if they conflict
with his or her own ideas.   _____
                                                                       10

3 —Tries to help subordinates understand company
objectives.   _____

—Lets subordinates figure out for themselves how
company objectives apply to them.   _____
                                                                       10

4 —Tries to give subordinates access to all the information
they want.   _____

—Gives subordinates the information he thinks they need.   _____
                                                                       10

5 —Tends to set subordinates' job goals and tell them how
to achieve them.   _____

—Involves subordinates in solving problems and setting
job goals.   _____
                                                                       10

6 —Tends to discourage subordinates from trying new
    approaches.   _____

  —Tries to encourage subordinates to reach out in new
    directions.   _____
                                                        10

7 —Takes your mistakes in stride, so long as you learn
    from them.   _____

  —Allows little room for mistakes, especially those that
    might embarrass him or her.   _____
                                                        10

8 —Tries mainly to correct mistakes and figures out how
    they can be prevented in the future.   _____

  —When something goes wrong, tries primarily to find out
    who caused it.   _____
                                                        10

9 —Expectations of subordinates tend to fluctuate. _____

  —Consistent, high expectations of subordinates.   _____
                                                        10

10—Expects superior performance and gives credit when
    you do it.   _____

  —Expects you to do an adequate job, doesn't say much
    unless something goes wrong.   _____
                                                        10

EXERCISE — RELATIONSHIP ANALYZER AND PLANNER

AM I NOW ...

• Directly involved in a difficult work relationship?

• Dissatisfied with the situation as it now stands?

• Willing to take the first steps toward initiating a change?

IF SO ...

• This set of worksheets is a self-questionnaire to help in analyzing that relationship. Answering its questions can help me discover what I can do. Since the
  fault must not be 100% in the other person's corner, I can be already well on
  my way to a better relationship.

NEXT . . .

• Make a working copy of Activities A, B, and C.

• Think about a particular person and recent encounters with him or her.

• Stop and reflect: what are my concerns, feelings, and plans about this?

• Now step back for perspective and carefully answer the worksheet questions.

• Consider checking your analysis with some objective party.

• Consider discussing the results of your analysis with the other person involved.

• Implement whatever action steps you come up with.

• Put your notes aside in a tickler file for later reference.

Activity A. Descriptive Analysis

What is happening now in the relationship between "A" and myself?

_____

_____

_____

_____

_____

_____

How does this person behave toward me, my ideas and my function?

_____

_____

_____

_____

_____

_____

How do I find myself reacting to this person, his or her ideas or function?

_____

_____

_____

_____

_____

_____

What are the issues/areas that seem to trigger our problems?

_____

_____

_____

_____

_____

_____

In general, how would I describe our relationship problems?

_____

_____

_____

_____

_____

With the relationship now described in general terms, I can proceed to look at specific aspects of it, as a next step to an effective solution.

_____

_____

_____

_____

_____

_____

Activity B. Contribution Analysis

How am I maintaining the difficulties and contributing to improvement?

• Consider *every* column in turn

• Check *every* box that seems relevant to the relationship described. Force an assessment on *each* column.

• Jot down in the checked boxes notes on the major things I do or ways I think that contribute to this degree of difficulty or excellence. Assess my strengths as well as my problems:

| Degree of Difficulty or Excellence | TYPES OF ACTIVITY IN THE RELATIONSHIP — Basic types of work activities that may be involved in this relationship are listed below. Any relationship may vary in effectiveness level across these activity areas. | | | | | | | | | |
	Coaching	Planning or Goal Setting	Giving Direction or Instructions	Information Sharing	Discipline Situations	Meetings or Group Situations	Working Together on Task	A Crisis or Problem Situation	Policy or Procedure Areas	Other
Severe strain/difficulties: Task accomplishments are blocked and/or inappropriate tensions and actions are maintained.										
Hard, but workable: It takes a real extra effort to overcome deficiencies in skill, attitudes or style, and get the work done.										
Excellent working relationship. In this aspect, the parties involved are adequately skilled, sensitive, and able to bring out the best in each other.										
Not Applicable:										

Activity C. Improvements

Applying the above Descriptive Analysis and Contribution Analysis to actual employees under your management or supervision, list actions you would like to take to:

1. Improve your perception of what employees think about you; and,

2. Improve relations with these employees.

PART II. SELF-ESTEEM

CONTENTS:

READING — THE SIGNIFICANCE OF SELF-ESTEEM

We have often discussed the value of introspection — the importance of knowing one's inner self. Today, we will focus on yet another requirement for mental well-being — the need for self-esteem. It is the regard we have for our own standing, or position in life, and as individuals, we have a responsibility to maintain our own self-esteem.

Psychologist Nathanial Brandon believes there is no value judgment more important to man, no factor more decisive in his psychological development and motivation, than the estimate he passes on himself. We are always evaluating our thoughts and actions; it is a natural, constant, part of life. Like anything else we do, it can be good or bad, creative or destructive. But, if self-esteem is going to benefit us, then our self-evaluation must be of a positive nature. We need self-esteem to make proper value judgments, for what we think of ourselves is in large measure responsible for what we do for ourselves. If we are going to achieve true happiness and success, we must respect ourselves and believe we are, indeed, worthy to enjoy life.

We must also be careful not to let emotions interfere with our reasoning powers. Brandon points out that the ability to distinguish between knowledge and feelings is an essential element in the process of a mind's healthy maturation. It is vital for the achievement and preservation of self-esteem.

Now, it is also important that we, as managers, recognize the role we can play in helping others build their self-esteem. Nothing will help us believe in ourselves faster than the knowledge that someone else holds us in high regard.

We recently mentioned the need to be needed. And, part of the reason for that is the self-esteem it builds. Yes, one of the greatest adventures in living is to get to know ourselves better. We must take time to make friends with ourselves, and we must begin believing in our own talent and special capabilities. If we do this, we will surely build our self-esteem.

As the great English writer, Aldous Huxley, wrote: "There is only one corner of the universe you can be certain of improving — and, that is your own self." (From a Mormon Tabernacle Broadcast — October 1974)

EXERCISE — QUESTIONNAIRE ON SELF-ESTEEM

	Agree	Don't Know	Disagree
1. I really feel as if I am a part of this organization.	_____	_____	_____
2. I am really doing something worthwhile in my job.	_____	_____	_____
3. I can learn a great deal on my present job.	_____	_____	_____
4. I have little opportunity to use my abilities in this department.	_____	_____	_____
5. I am proud to work for this department.	_____	_____	_____

6. How do you feel about:

	Completely Unsatisfactory			Fully Satisfactory
a. The opportunity for independent thought and action in your position.	1	2	3	4
b. The feeling of self-esteem you get from being in your position.	1	2	3	4
c. The opportunity for personal growth and development in your position.	1	2	3	4

58

		Small			Very Important
d. The feeling of self-fulfillment you get from being in your position.	1		2	3	4
e. The feeling of worthwhile ac- complishment in your position.	1		2	3	4

	Small			Very Important
7. How much of a share do you feel you have in determining the success of your department?	1		2	3	4

READING — AS YOU WERE SAYING . . .

Personal Motivation — The Secret of Success

Personal motivation means the development of inner strength, conscious willpower, overwhelming desire and the determination to reach any goal that *you*, personally, want to achieve. It is the most important prerequisite to success in any endeavor, according to Paul J. Meyer, president of Success Motivation, Inc. In his opinion, this ability isn't inherited but comes from within and is a quality that all of us possess to a greater or lesser degree.

How do you motivate yourself? Where do you begin? Meyer suggests that you start with a frank, honest self-appraisal and ask yourself these questions:

Where Do I Stand Now?

Evaluate your strengths and your weaknesses, your assets and liabilities. Put the answers down in black and white — to show *exactly where you stand now*. Face yourself squarely, honestly, realistically.

What Are My Goals?

Do you have any definite aims or goals? Do you know what you really want in each of the six most important areas of your life?

By "six most important areas," I mean physically, spiritually, mentally, finan- cially, socially and your home and family life.

Do you know what your short-range goals are . . . your long-range goals . . . your tangible goals . . . your intangible goals . . . in each of these six areas?

After you've answered these questions you may still ask, "How do I motivate myself? How can I become successful through personal motivation?"

Crystalize Your Thinking

Determine what specific goals you want to achieve — short-range, long-range, tangible and intangible — then write this information down.

Writing crystalizes thought and thought motivates action. Be specific about your goals; don't generalize or use vague terms. Use vivid imagination. *Picturize.* We must develop the faculty of seeing with our mind's eye; seeing concisely, exactly what we imagine.

There is a universal law: "We tend to draw to ourselves that which we set out from ourselves." No man can attract to himself what his thought repels. We become precisely that which we imagine ourselves to be. Low aim is only low self-concept expressing itself. When your goals are clear and vivid, they act as a magnet to draw you to them.

Goal setting is the most important positive action of your life. When you've written this down, *dedicate* yourself to its attainment. Do this with honest zeal and singleness of purpose and with unswerving one-trackmanship.

Develop A Plan for Achieving Your Goal and A Deadline for Its Attainment

This detailed plan is the road map, the design, that will guide you to your goal. The plan must necessarily list the obstacles and the roadblocks between where you are now and where you want to go and, also, how you intend to get around them, through them or over them.

Be frank with yourself; remember your strengths and your weaknesses, your assets and your liabilities. Write them out, just as you did with your goals. Also, write down very clearly your way around the obstacles and the roadblocks.

Then make a specific schedule of time organization — a detailed outline of the progress you intend to make. Put down every step and move — day-by-day, week-by-week, month-by-month — you'll need them to check on the progress you're making.

Develop A Sincere Desire for the Things You Want in Life

A burning desire is the greatest motivator of every human action. Unquestionably, the degree of success you achieve depends on the amount of sincere desire you have.

Desire is akin to thirst. When you've visualized exactly what you want in each area of your life, desire will add strength to your purpose; it will improve your self-image. Also at this point, you can determine the very real difference between "wish" and "desire." You can discover the difference easily by asking yourself these three questions:

1. What are the obstacles and roadblocks I will have to overcome to achieve my goals?

2. What are the rewards if I attain them?

3. Is it worth it to me?

If your answer is "yes," you'll know you have genuine *desire.*

Develop Confidence in Yourself and Your Own Abilities

Confidence in yourself helps you to deal honestly with your shortcomings and compels you to make consistent corrections.

Confidence comes from experience. Experience comes from know-how. Know-how comes from having the courage to submit yourself to obstacles, situations and circumstances that the average person shies away from. People who lack confidence are not goal directed but stand on the sidelines as passive bystanders.

Confidence stimulates your creative imagination. No matter what you undertake, you will *never* do it until you think you can. You will never master it until you have the confidence in yourself to do the deed first in your own mind. It must be mentally accomplished before it can be materially accomplished.

The primary element at the beginning of any enterprise — the one factor which will guarantee its success — is *confidence* that it can be done.

Develop A Dogged Determination to Follow Through on Your Plan.

Determination is persistency. If you make a decision, plan a course of action or make a resolution, but then ignore your intention, you'll form a habit of failure. When you make up your mind to follow your plan of personal motivation — do it! Let nothing or no one interfere.

You can further develop your determination by reviewing your written plan often, by concentrating on the rewards. Thus, your desire and determination will stimulate a flow of dynamic and positive direction to keep you on course until your aims are realized.

A person who is success minded has a success consciousness and success awareness; he lives with positive expectancy. He lives by the law of attraction. He magnetizes his condition.

When you apply these five points in a plan for your own personal motivation, when you develop success attitudes and success habits and have a plan of action, you'll find yourself living with positive expectancy!

EXERCISE — PERSONAL MOTIVATION AND GOALS
PURPOSE

- To illustrate how particular goals are the basis for own behavior.
- To provide a framework for goal-setting with employees.

PROCEDURE
(Time: 30 minutes)

- Review "Personal Motivation — The Secret of Success."
- Next, jot down two of your specific goals (job or home related) and *work backwards* tracing these through using the following categories:

   a) What is the need(s) that is not completely satisfied?

   b) What specific behavior is the result of this need?

Complete the following chart using two of your specific goals:

	NEEDS ➡	BEHAVIOR ➡	GOALS
1.			
2.			

Now select one of your employees and trace through one of their goals using the same chart:

	NEEDS ➡	BEHAVIOR ➡	GOALS

PART III. REWARDS

CONTENTS:

Reading — The Right Reward for the Right Reason to the Right Individual or Group

Exercise — Evaluation of Your Company's Reward Programs

READING — THE RIGHT REWARD FOR THE RIGHT REASON
TO THE RIGHT INDIVIDUAL OR GROUP

Fair and creditable rewards are essential to sustaining effective involvement of people to improve quality and productivity, as well as other company operations. Most companies have evolved several forms of reward programs over the years for reasons that seemed right at the time. Many may remain creditable. Others probably need revision. Some should be cancelled. The subject is so important that a separate chapter on communication and rewards has been included later in the book.

It is the intent, now, to evaluate your company's reward programs to determine if they are the right programs for the right reasons, and if the rewards are being given to the right individuals or groups.

Below are ten forms of rewards which are "right" rewards if given for the right reason:

10 REWARDS	TO REWARD	INSTEAD OF
1. Money	1. Solid solutions	1. Quick fixes
2. Recognition	2. Risk taking	2. Risk avoiding
3. Time off	3. Applied creativity	3. Mindless conformity
4. A piece of the action	4. Decisive action	4. Paralysis by analysis
5. Favorite work	5. Smart work	5. Busywork
6. Advancement	6. Simplification	6. Needless complication
7. Freedom	7. Quietly effective behavior	7. Squeaking joints
8. Personal growth	8. Quality work	8. Fast work
9. Fun	9. Loyalty	9. Turnover
10. Prizes	10. Working together	10. Working against

For distinction between rewards for the right reason and those for the wrong reason are given in the following list of "Solid Solutions" versus "Quick Fixes."

A SOLID SOLUTION IS:	A QUICK FIX IS:
1. Making a commitment to a long-range plan and staying with it.	1. Achieving short-run goals at any cost.
2. Regularly retooling and investing in new and better ways to get things done.	2. Using old equipment until it falls apart because that's the cheapest way to go.
3. Treating employees the way you would like to be treated. Investing in the growth and development of an ongoing, committed, well-trained team.	3. Hiring and firing employees as needed.

4. Committing to the development of new and better products and services because innovation is any business's greatest capital asset.

4. Avoiding the development of new products and services unless the payoff is high and the risk is low.

5. Having customer service that generates repeat business.

5. Trying to make a bundle on one quick sale.

6. Maintaining fair and stable prices that generate customer trust and loyalty.

6. Raising and lowering prices to reach current profit goals.

7. Acquiring only those businesses the company has the skills to manage.

7. Venturing into a new industry because the financial gurus promise fast payoff with low risk.

8. Rewarding people, through an ongoing program, for finding ways to work more efficiently.

8. Slashing expenses to the bone in a cost-cutting drive.

9. Emphasizing quality as the key to improving productivity.

9. Delivering the goods on time at any cost.

10. Realizing that the people closest to the job usually know most about it and tapping their brain power.

10. Letting managers make all the decisions because it is faster and they are paid to do so.

It sometimes happens that rewards are granted to individuals or groups for social or political reasons instead of only to those who earned them. This is a vital evaluation criterion.

Another consideration in the design of reward programs has to do with the Hierarchy of Human Needs described in Figures 3.4 and 3.5. Distinctions are made between employee psychological and safety needs that are not real motivators; social needs that are minimal motivators; and ego and self-actualization needs that are high motivators. The reader should review these figures.

EXERCISE — EVALUATION OF YOUR COMPANY'S REWARD PROGRAMS

Procedure

1. List your company's reward programs.
2. Using the criteria provided in the reading assignment, evaluate each of your company programs as follows:
   a. Compare your programs with the forms of rewards given in the reading assignment and list the number of these forms where there is similarity.

b. For each company program, evaluate if actual rewards are given for the right or wrong reasons by noting: mostly yes, sometimes yes, sometimes no, and mostly no. Supplement with comments.

c. Using the criteria for solid solutions versus quick fixes in the reading assignment, select the behavior from each column that sounds most like where you work and circle it.

d. Evaluate your company's programs on whether rewards are given to the right individuals or groups by indicating: all the time, most of the time, over half the time, or less than half the time. Supplement with comments.

e. Evaluate your programs with the criteria from the Hierachy of Human Needs by indicating for each factor low, medium or high motivation programs.

"New Basic" — Development and application of manager's skills to improve environments, management style, and attitudes to enable more effective involvement and management of employees.

CHAPTER 5
THE MANAGEMENT WORKSHOP CONTINUES
Improving Attitudes, Environments And Management Characteristics

This chapter continues to teach skills about how to apply the first, and most important, "new basic": the development and application of manager's skills to improve environments, management style, and attitudes that enables more effective involvement and management of employees.

PART I. ATTITUDES

CONTENTS:

Reading — Ways to Learn Existing Attitudes and Improve Them

Exercise — Individual Differences and Uniqueness

Reading — The Nondirective Interview — A One-On-One Technique for Learning Attitudes

Exercises — Conducting a Nondirective Interview
Interfacing

READING — WAYS TO LEARN EXISTING ATTITUDES
AND IMPROVE THEM

The process begins by determining the attitudes that exist within the company. Accurate means have been developed to learn the existing attitudes of middle and front line managers, professional personnel, technicians, supervisors and hourly employees. Attitude surveys conducted by third party professionals do this. Most attitude surveys are designed using either the Likert-Type Scale or the Thurston Scale. Examples of both scales follow. In addition, reviews of exit interviews and appraisal interviews reveal attitudes.

The top official usually does not have these tools to determine the attitudes of his top managers. Other information is often available from the process of searching, interviewing and hiring the individual, from first hand experience working with him, and from other sources. In the process of developing a company philosophy and balanced company objectives that benefit both company and employees, new attitudes often emerge.

To change attitudes requires the patience and skills of a diplomat, the persistence of a bulldog and the subtlety of a Japanese manager. At the beginning, it must be recognized that each individual is different and has different points of view. Ways to improve attitudes include:

- Realizing every individual is different and must be dealt with accordingly.
- Changing facts to improve opinions.
- Making each employee feel he is a vital part of a group.
- Role playing.
- Use of listening skills.
- Use of discussion skills.

In the usual situation, there are many individuals with open minds, who, despite vested interests, are willing to listen to new ideas for change and to reach objective opinions. Occasionally there is the individual who by nature is against change and tends to dig in his heels. The best approach is to influence the open-minded individuals initially and let the peer process help influence the inhibitor.

As a practical consideration, it is worth noting that there is often one top manager who possesses an attitude of dominance and mistrust, cloaked in a suit labeled "hard-headed manager." This person can extend his shadow deep within an organization and generate undesirable attitudes. Terminating or transferring this individual to work that does not affect others often results in more positive changes in employee attitudes than the many suggestions given here. There is nothing wrong about "hard-headed" or "tough" management that is objective and fair and not warped by deep insecurity or dictatorial aspirations. Employees can tell the difference.

Top management can contribute the most to changing attitudes. They can start with development of the company philosophy and objectives that put meaning to the phrase often heard by employees — "our employees are our most important product." Their leadership of the effort described in this book provides the examples.

Openness in providing the results of attitude surveys to employees creates credibility with employees. Informing them of "quick fixes" reduces this credibility, while carefully developed — and usually longer range — responses to findings reinforce credibility.

Middle managers can be the key factor in improving attitudes or preventing improvement. Attitude is a "top-down" proposition. Someone must have an idea to make a major change and it is often the top official. If not, he must be convinced and make a commitment. He must learn and often change the attitudes of his top managers. But, early in the game, top management must enable middle management to become involved. It is essential that their attitudes are learned and changed where necessary before further success is possible. Middle management is a major hurdle.

The bottom line is that efforts to improve quality and productivity through more effective use of employees must await perception by the employees that credible action is underway to improve the environment and attend to their real needs. Completion of the effort to improve the environment is not necessary. But speeches, announcements, letters and posters do not trigger significant change in attitudes.

They only trigger curiosity. Employees are quick to recognize actions. They are also quick to want to participate in the processes of improving the environment, products, services and systems.

Attitude Surveys

The Likert-Type Scale

Likert has also contributed the "Likert-Type Scale." It is one of the most widely used scales in social research. The Management Workshop and the Supervisor Training Program make extensive use of the scale. It involves making a statement about an important issue, person, or characteristic. A person's reaction or opinion can be indicated by selecting one of several possible responses, ranging from extremes in both directions to neutral, or no reaction/opinion. Figure 5.1A provides examples.

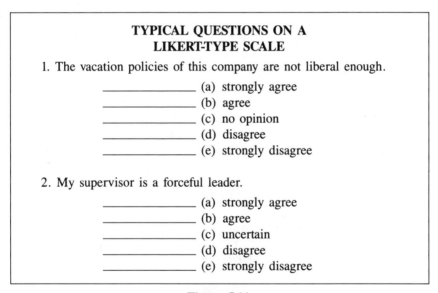

**TYPICAL QUESTIONS ON A
LIKERT-TYPE SCALE**

1. The vacation policies of this company are not liberal enough.

   _____ (a) strongly agree
   _____ (b) agree
   _____ (c) no opinion
   _____ (d) disagree
   _____ (e) strongly disagree

2. My supervisor is a forceful leader.

   _____ (a) strongly agree
   _____ (b) agree
   _____ (c) uncertain
   _____ (d) disagree
   _____ (e) strongly disagree

Figure 5.1A

The Thurston Scale

A large number of statements are generated bearing on any topic on which attitude is to be measured. The statements are analyzed to assure that they are not ambiguous but that they are diagnostic in representing a position for or against the issue involved. The best statements are retained and assigned a scale value, such as between 0 and 12. Those statements that strongly favor the issue receive a high value. Statements strongly opposed receive low values. Those in between are given intermediate values. Note that the degree of favorableness of each statement declines as one goes down the list in the example below.

Thurston Scale

STATEMENT	SCALE VALUE
I think this company treats its employees better than any other company does	10.4
If I had to do it over again, I'd still work for this company	9.5
They don't play favorites in this company	9.3
A man can get ahead in this company if he tries	9.3
I have as much confidence in the company physician as I do in my own doctor	8.7
The company is sincere in wanting to know what its employees think about it	8.5
A wage-incentive plan offers a just reward for the faster worker	7.9
On the whole, the company treats us about as well as we deserve	7.4
I think a man should go to the hospital for even a scratch as it may prevent blood poisoning	6.3
I believe accidents will happen, no matter what you do about them	5.4
The workers put as much over on the company as the company puts over on them	5.1
The company does too much welfare work	4.4
Soldiering on the job is increasing	4.1
I do not think applicants for employment are treated courteously	3.6
I believe many good suggestions are killed by the bosses	3.2
My boss gives all the breaks to his lodge and church friends	2.9
I think the company goes outside to fill good jobs instead of promoting men who are here	2.5
You've got to have "pull" with certain people around here to get ahead	2.1
In the long run this company will "put it over" on you	1.5
The pay in this company is terrible	1.0
An honest man fails in this company	0.8

Figure 5.1B

**Desired Changes In Attitudes Of Managers
And Supervisors Toward Employees**

From	*To*
Dominance	Cooperation
Rejection	Acceptance
Mistrust	Confidence
Defensive	Open-minded
Phony	Sincere
Apathetic	Enthusiastic
Critical	Helpful

Individual Differences

In any study of motivation and interactions, the first important psychological principle to be considered is that *every individual is different in almost every respect from every other individual.* In the rather natural attempt to simplify and expedite dealings with others, we attempt to neatly classify and label individuals as fitting into clear-cut categories to which we can apply standardized approaches and treatment so as to reach the desired goals. We assume that the approach which was successful with one or more individuals will be suitable for all others. It is necessary for us to realize that seeking such generalized approaches in motivation rather than adapting them to the individual is apt to lead to poor or inept performance in dealing with others.

Thus, the engineer who attempts to approach all supervisors or hourly rated workers in an unvarying, highly routinized manner; the manager who feels that all of his personnel can be highly motivated by an occasional, perfunctory compliment; and the manager who thinks all hourly rated individuals have the same hostile attitude toward him and his work — all are reducing their efficiency in dealing with people. The importance of being aware of individual differences can perhaps be emphasized by stating that not even identical twins can be dealt with in exactly the same manner, for they often vary decidedly in such important characteristics as personality, feelings of security or insecurity, or in the motivations that control their activities.

In taking a closer look at this subject of *individual differences,* it is apparent they fall into *two major groups.* The one group would include those which deal mainly with the *physical and mental capacities* or skills which an individual may possess. The second group concerns itself mainly with the *psychological or social differences,* especially as they manifest themselves in personality traits. Both of these groups are intimately related and both must be kept in mind when attempting to interact with any given individual. An obvious example of this relationship would be the marked personality traits which are often developed by individuals who have a physical deformity.

The important thing to remember about the hereditary traits and capacities of the individual is that they set the limits to which skills can be developed in these areas. Even the best training cannot give an individual a higher level of intelligence or better muscular coordination than he has inherited. In these respects, therefore, it is important that not more is expected of an individual than he is capable of delivering. Also, this capacity cannot be developed where it is not present in the hereditary structure of the individual.

Motivation

One of the most important areas in which we find wide variations in individuals is that of *motivation.* Motivation can best be defined as the wishes or desires an individual has to enter into certain activities which lead to desired goals. It is necessary to remember at all times that every act or form of behavior of an individual is motivated. No form of behavior is without some sort of purpose or goal even though such a goal may be only vaguely defined in the thinking of the individual concerned. This definition points out the importance of recognizing and understanding motivation in dealing with others. This includes our own motivations as well as the motivations of others. One cannot understand or attempt to modify the behavior of others without some knowledge of their motivations.

The origin of motivations and their role in behavior can best be portrayed in the following formula:

Needs $\longrightarrow$ Motives $\longrightarrow$ Behavior $\longrightarrow$ Goals

Here it is seen that motives must arise from feelings of need on the part of the individual. Once an individual becomes aware of a need or set of needs, he seeks to establish a goal which will remove or satisfy this need. When the goal is established, the wish or desire is formed to obtain the goal. This wish then sets up and energizes the behavior which will supposedly obtain the goal. This motive will cease to exist only when the need ceases to exist or is satisfied. It is somewhat difficult to observe motives in another person since they are by definition a mental state and can be observed only indirectly through the behavior of the individual concerned.

EXERCISE — INDIVIDUAL DIFFERENCES AND UNIQUENESS

Individual Work (10 minutes)

• List on a piece of paper the five or six key things (people, experiences, tasks, etc.) in your life that have had the most influence on you to cause you to be in your present occupation.

• List on a piece of paper your unique qualities as a person.

Small Group Work (15 minutes)

• In triads share with each other the items you have written down in response to the above tasks.

READING — THE NONDIRECTIVE INTERVIEW
A One-On-One Technique For Learning Attitudes

The technique of "reflecting feelings" involves about 90% listening. The other 10% is responding in such a way that you, the interviewer, are not imposing the direction the interview takes, but are following the lead of the interviewee. It is as if you are holding up a mirror which is very special that allows facts, data and detailed descriptions of situations or events to pass through, and reflects only feelings, hopes, fears, irritations and disappointments.

There are certain rules which an individual who follows the reflecting feelings approach must observe. These are:

1. Preface every attempt to reflect feelings with such phrases as:
   you feel ...
   you believe ...
   you think ...   (or similar phrases)
   you hope ...
   you fear ...

2. Reflect back feelings as statements, not as questions.

3. Restate feelings in your own words — paraphrase don't parrot.

4. *Wait out pauses.*

5. After a long speech, reflect only *last feeling* expressed.

6. Don't reflect feelings until they are *explicitly expressed* — don't jump ahead or anticipate.

7. Don't make extrapolations and follow logical deductions.

8. *Avoid answering questions.* If the person persists in asking questions, you may not be in a nondirective situation.

9. Use a neutral tone of voice, one that is not critical, apologetic, sarcastic or disapproving.

10. Facial expressions should also be kept neutral.

EXERCISE — CONDUCTING A NONDIRECTIVE INTERVIEW

The purpose of this practice session is to evaluate the impact and effectiveness of a nondirective approach as an aid to help an individual get at the root of a problem and find a possible solution. This technique represents an approach which you could use in working with the employees who report to you to help them solve problems they face at work. Use the approach and observe what happens.

You will work in groups of three. For the purposes of this exercise, one of you will be the individual with the problem. The second will be the interviewer who will use a nondirective approach to help the individual reach a way to solve the problem. The third will be an observer who will record what went on during the interview, what techniques the interviewer used and how well or poorly they worked.

Your time should be allocated as follows:

Review and prepare for the interview	5 minutes
Conduct the interview	10 minutes
Discussion	10 minutes

EXERCISE — INTERFACING

Interviewer's Instructions

The individual with whom you will be talking has identified, during the preparation time, a problem he currently faces. Structure your approach so that you allow this individual to discuss the problem freely, without fear of criticism or penalty. Make it possible for him to talk about the *feelings* he has about the current situation and any frustration or emotion he is experiencing. Your goal is to make it possible for him to talk through the problem in such a way that he may be able to perceive it in a somewhat different manner which will lead him to a possible solution.

Draw on the ideas and techniques which we have been discussing about nondirective interviewing. Remember the ten rules about how to reflect feelings. Avoid violating these rules. To be sure, there are other techniques which help individuals talk more easily. But try, for purposes of this practice session, to focus on the use of the nondirective approach. You are seeking ways to help the individual shed more information on the problem so that he may develop a solution. Refrain from any action, verbal or nonverbal, which prevents him from talking about actions he has taken or is thinking about trying to solve the problem.

As a manager, your first impulse will be to jump in and tell him what to do. But don't. Use the nondirective technique to let him come up with a solution.

1. *Individual Task*
   Identify key interface situations which you face in carrying out your management role. (List as many as you can.)
   (Time: 5 minutes)

2. Rank in terms of priority of action the top four interface areas that represent motivational situations for you.
   (Time: 5 minutes)

3. Based on all of the things we have talked about in this course:
   a. Identify the *specific actions* you are willing to commit yourself to at this time for these four top areas.
   b. Indicate *when* these actions will take place and *who* will carry them out.
   c. Since these actions are important, and possibly difficult — think about and write down the names of *other people* who may help you carry them out.
   (Time: 30 minutes)

Note: You will be asked to share these proposed action items with the rest of the group. Be prepared to present your plans in a brief, crisp manner.

PART II. TRUST — OPENNESS — SELF-CONTROL

CONTENTS:

READING — POSITIVE ENVIRONMENTAL ELEMENTS

McGregor

- Theory Y is an invitation to innovation, and an environment associated with Theory Y likewise requires innovation.

- It is an environment of trust which changes by degree from a centralized management control and regulation of employees to one which permits greater self-regulation.

- It is an environment to get more out of people by allowing them greater freedom to voluntarily contribute more of their abilities to their tasks.

- It is an environment which associates company goals with the self-interest and growth of the employee.

- It is an environment which permits the organization to be propelled by employee motivation rather than using the organization to suppress that motivation.

- It is an environment that provides an attitude of helpfulness rather than dominance and guidance rather than control.

Zand

- Realistic communication and shared goals.
- Cooperative attitude between related organizational groups.
- Trust and openness.
- High quality-production goals established in part by employees.

Hughes

- An environment of trust which changes by degree from a centralized management control and regulation of employees to one which permits self-regulation.
- An environment to get more out of people by allowing them greater freedom to contribute voluntarily more of their abilities to their tasks.
- An environment which associates company goals with the self-interest and growth of the employee.
- An environment that provides an attitude of helpfulness rather than dominance and of guidance rather than control.
- Such conditions as freedom to speak, freedom to do what one wishes so long as no harm is done to others, freedom to express oneself, freedom to investigate and seek information, freedom to defend oneself, justice, fairness, honesty, and orderliness in the group are examples of such preconditions for basic need satisfactions.
- Realistic communication and shared goals; increased informal communication, where appropriate.
- Cooperative attitude between related organizational groups.
- Trust and openness.

READING — NEGATIVE ENVIRONMENTAL ELEMENTS

McGregor

- An environment of management vigilance over human beings who are assumed to be pious, permanently arrested in their own development and of limited individual initiative and ability, such as the factory hand of the past.
- An environment which keeps the implied threat of unemployment handy in case it is needed.
- An environment which does cater to security needs and obvious fringe benefits but is quite autocratic and possibly dogmatic.

Zand

- Communication of minimum goals.
- Employee's standard is self-protection.
- Fear and hostility.
- Strong top-side control.
- Lack of confidence.
- Playing it "close to the chest."

EXERCISE — A COMBINED CRITERION FOR
POSITIVE ENVIRONMENTAL ELEMENTS

There exists a reasonable consensus by the experts on positive environmental elements. They obviously agree on most elements, but they say it in different ways. The criterion is less confusing if the experts' views can be combined and consolidated.

This exercise asks you to:

1. Prepare a combined and consolidated criteria of the positive environmental elements.

2. Compare your list with other lists in the group and develop an agreed-upon expression of the criterion.

EXERCISE — NEGATIVE ENVIRONMENTAL ELEMENTS LISTING

There exists a reasonable consensus by the experts about environmental elements that demotivate and should be corrected if they exist or avoided if they don't exist. We have selected two as being representative. A single listing is more readily usable than multiple lists that say about the same thing but in different ways.

1 . Prepare a combined and consolidated list of negative environmental elements to be avoided.

2. Compare with other lists in the group and develop an agreed-upon expression of the list.

EXERCISE — THE EXISTING ENVIRONMENT FOR
YOUR COMPANY
Using The Likert Scale

1. For each positive environmental criteria from the first exercise, apply the Likert Scale (see Figure 5.1A) following the example below:

The criteria for this individual positive environmental element is met in my company.

_____ a. strongly agree

_____ b. agree

_____ c. uncertain

_____ d. disagree

_____ e. strongly disagree

2. Discuss and compare with the group.

EXERCISE — YOUR COMPANY AND NEGATIVE
ENVIRONMENTAL ELEMENTS

1. For each negative element in the list from the second exercise, apply the Likert Scale following the example below:

    This individual negative environmental element exists in our company.

    _____ a. strongly agree
    _____ b. agree
    _____ c. uncertain
    _____ d. disagree
    _____ e. strongly disagree

2. Discuss and compare with the group.

EXERCISE — AGREE-DISAGREE

Individually complete this scale prior to the group task such that it represents *your* personal feelings.

> *Please circle the number on the agree-disagree scale*
> *which best reflects your opinion of each statement.*

1. A clear cut hierarchy of authority is essential in a business organization.

1	2	3	4	5	6	7	8	9
Strongly							Strongly	
agree							disagree	

2. Money is the most effective motivator of people.

9	8	7	6	5	4	3	2	1
Strongly							Strongly	
disagree							agree	

3. A manager should be a strong individualist.

1	2	3	4	5	6	7	8	9
Strongly							Strongly	
agree							disagree	

4. A manager must weigh very carefully what kinds of information he shares with subordinates.

9	8	7	6	5	4	3	2	1
Strongly							Strongly	
disagree							agree	

5. Persons paid to assume the responsibility should personally carry the burden of decision making.

9	8	7	6	5	4	3	2	1

Strongly
disagree

Strongly
agree

6. Being firm with employees is the best way to insure that they will do a good job.

1	2	3	4	5	6	7	8	9

Strongly
agree

Strongly
disagree

7. The most effective way to get people motivated and committed to a job is to instruct, direct and use appropriate rewards and penalties.

9	8	7	6	5	4	3	2	1

Strongly
disagree

Strongly
agree

8. Individual decisions are consistently more sound than group decisions.

1	2	3	4	5	6	7	8	9

Strongly
agree

Strongly
disagree

9. All work groups need a single leader.

1	2	3	4	5	6	7	8	9

Strongly
agree

Strongly
disagree

10. Most people are basically dependent and want their thoughts to be directed by those who know more.

9	8	7	6	5	4	3	2	1

Strongly
disagree

Strongly
agree

Please sum up the numbers you have circled for
all ten statements and write the total here: ☐

PART III. MANAGEMENT CHARACTERISTICS

CONTENTS:

Reading — The Evolution of Managerial Style in a Typical Company

Exercise — Profiling Using Evolution of Management Style in a Typical Company

Reading — Likert's Management Characteristics

Exercise — Profiling Using Likert's Management Characteristics

READING — THE EVOLUTION OF MANAGERIAL STYLE IN A TYPICAL COMPANY

	1.	2.	3.	4.
Tasks	Simple, requires no group interactions.	Simple most of the time; sometimes complex; no group interaction.	Complex, requiring a *low* degree of group interaction.	Complex, requiring a *high* degree of group interaction.
Business Environment	Stable with minor risks.	Changing but little competition.	Rapidly changing with increasing competition.	Rapidly changing, highly complex and increasing risks.
The Era of . . .	Industrial engineering and task simplification	The Personnel Man and the Party Giver	The P.R. man and scientist working alone	The planner, the team builder, and the systems engineer
Motivating Force	Pressure from management.	Subordinate gratitude for social needs being met.	Subordinates highly committed to personal tasks.	Group commitment to a group task.
Psychological Environment	Hard working but resentful under management pressure.	Social atmosphere.	Frantic, anxious, confused.	Hard working under internalized and peer group pressure.
Subordinates — Technically	Unskilled.	Skilled.	Skilled and professional.	Highly skilled and professionally competent.
Subordinates — Psychologically	Want material needs met.	Want social needs met.	Want opportunities to perform and prove oneself, i.e., recognition.	Want opportunities to be of service and a sense of accomplishment.

Subordinates expected to be	Obedient and hard working.	Happy.	Totally committed and able to correct problems with minimal or no organizational assistance.	Work the problems with organizational help.
Leaders — Technically	Knowledgeable about task of each subordinate.	Knowledgeable about most tasks of subordinates.	Not knowledgeable about tasks.	Knowledgeable about goals to be accomplished.
Leaders — Psychologically	Authoritative; make all decisions; authority retained.	Appeasing, calculative.	Defensive. Makes few decisions. Authority retained. Responsibility up for grabs.	Open. Helps group make group decisions. Authority shared. Responsibility shared.
Management's Responsibility	Plan and organize.	Maintain friendly relationships and keep people happy.	Provide a challenge and then stay out of the way so people can work. See that people have a lot of tasks and always have less than what they need so organizational resources are not being wasted. Serve as a communicator to pass on some information.	Help the group to set goals. Facilitate the group process. Accept responsibility for effective group functioning rather than subordinate's responsibility. Practice the art of integrating subordinate's goals with organizational objectives.

Figure 5.2

EXERCISE — EVOLUTION OF MANAGERIAL STYLE
IN A TYPICAL COMPANY

Individual Work

5 min. Take a few minutes to review the reading, "The Evolution of Managerial Style. . . "

5 min. Starting with the first item (Tasks), place a check mark in the column that best describes your organization (typically at department or plant level) at the present time. Next check a column in Business Environment category, etc.

Group Work

15 min. As a group, arrive at general agreement as to which column best represents your organization (typically at department or plant level) in each item category.

15 min. On chart paper, list the major conclusions and/or things learned by your group.

Bring your charts back to main conference room for a brief report. (Please limit your reports to major conclusions and things learned.)

40 min. total time for exercise.

READING – LIKERT'S MANAGEMENT CHARACTERISTICS

Organizational and Performance Characteristics of Different Management Systems Based on a Comparative Analysis

Figure 5.3

	System of organization			
	Authoritative		Consultative	Participative
Organizational variable	Exploitative authoritative System 1	Benevolent authoritative System 2	Consultative System 3	Participative group System 4
1. Leadership processes used.				
Extent to which superiors have confidence and trust in subordinates	Have no confidence and trust in subordinates	Have condescending confidence and trust, such as master has to servant	Substantial but not complete confidence and trust; still wishes to keep control of decisions	Complete confidence and trust in all matters
Extent to which superiors behave so that subordinates feel free to discuss important things about their jobs with their immediate superior	Subordinates do not feel at all free to discuss things about the job with their superior	Subordinates do not feel very free to discuss things about the job with their superior	Subordinates feel rather free to discuss things about the job with their superior	Subordinates feel completely free to discuss things about the job with their superior
Extent to which immediate superior in solving job problems generally tries to get subordinates' ideas and opinions and make constructive use of them	Seldom gets ideas and opinions of subordinates in solving job problems	Sometimes gets ideas and opinions of subordinates in solving job problems	Usually gets ideas and opinions and usually tries to make constructive use of them	Always gets ideas and opinions and always tries to make constructive use of them

LIKERT'S MANAGEMENT CHARACTERISTICS

Organizational and Performance Characteristics of Different Management Systems Based on a Comparative Analysis

Figure 5.3 (Continued)

Organizational variable	System of organization			
	Authoritative		Consultative	Participative
	Exploitative authoritative System 1	Benevolent authoritative System 2	Consultative System 3	Participative group System 4
2. Character of motivational forces.				
Manner in which motives are used	Fear, threats, punishment, and occasional rewards	Rewards and some actual or potential punishment	Rewards, occasional punishment, and some involvement	Economic rewards based on compensation system developed through participation; group participation and involvement in setting goals, improving methods, appraising progress toward goals, etc.
Amount of responsibility felt by each member of organization for achieving organization's goals	High levels of management feel responsibility; lower levels feel less; rank and file feel little and often welcome opportunity to behave in ways to defeat organization's goals	Managerial personnel usually feel responsibility; rank and file usually feel relatively little responsibility for achieving organization's goals	Substantial proportion of personnel, especially at high levels, feel responsibility and generally behave in ways to achieve the organization's goals	Personnel at all levels feel real responsibility for organization's goals and behave in ways to implement them

3. Character of communication process.

Amount of interaction and communication aimed at achieving organization's objectives	Very little	Little	Quite a bit	Much with both individuals and groups
Direction of information flow	Downward	Mostly downward	Down and up	Down, up, and with peers
Extent to which downward communications are accepted by subordinates	Viewed with great suspicion	May or may not be viewed with suspicion	Often accepted but at times viewed with suspicion; may or may not be openly questioned	Generally accepted, but if not, openly and candidly questioned
Accuracy of upward communication via line	Tends to be inaccurate	Information that boss wants to hear flows; other information is restricted and filtered	Information that boss wants to hear flows; other information may be limited or cautiously given	Accurate
Psychological closeness of superiors to subordinates (i.e., how well does superior know and understand problems faced by subordinates?)	Has no knowledge or understanding of problems of subordinates	Has some knowledge and understanding of problems of subordinates	Knows and understands problems of subordinates quite well	Knows and understands problems of subordinates very well

4. Character of interaction-influence process.

Amount and character of interaction	Little interaction and always with fear and distrust	Little interaction and usually with some condescension by superiors; fear and caution by subordinates	Moderate interaction, often with fair amount of confidence and trust	Extensive, friendly interaction with high degree of confidence and trust
Amount of cooperative teamwork present	None	Relatively little	A moderate amount	Very substantial amount throughout the organization

85

LIKERT'S MANAGEMENT CHARACTERISTICS

Organizational and Performance Characteristics of Different Management Systems Based on a Comparative Analysis

Figure 5.3 (Continued)

Organizational variable	System of organization			
	Authoritative		Participative	
	Exploitative authoritative System 1	Benevolent authoritative System 2	Consultative System 3	Participative group System 4
5. Character of decision-making process.				
At what level in organization are decisions formally made?	Bulk of decisions at top of organization	Policy at top, many decisions within prescribed framework made at lower levels	Broad policy and general decisions at top, more specific decisions at lower levels	Decision making widely done throughout organization, although well integrated through linking process provided by overlapping groups
To what extent are decision makers aware of problems, particularly those at lower levels in the organization?	Often are unaware or only partially aware	Aware of some, unaware of others	Moderately aware of problems	Generally quite well aware of problems
Extent to which technical and professional knowledge is used in decision making	Used only if possessed at higher levels	Much of what is available in higher and middle levels is used	Much of what is available in higher, middle and lower levels is used	Most of what is available anywhere in the organization is used

86

To what extent are subordinates involved in decisions related to their work?	Not at all	Never involved in decisions; occasionally consulted	Usually are consulted but ordinarily not involved in the decision making	Are involved fully in all decisions related to their work
Are decisions made at the best level in the organization so far as the motivational consequences (i.e., does the decision-making process help to create the necessary motivations in those persons who have to carry out the decisions?)	Decision making contributes little or nothing to the motivation to implement the decision, usually yields adverse motivation	Decision making contributes relatively little motivation	Some contribution by decision making to motivation to implement	Substantial contribution by decision-making processes to motivation to implement
6. Character of goal setting or ordering. Manner in which usually done	Orders issued	Orders issued, opportunity to comment may or may not exist	Goals are set or orders issued after discussion with subordinate(s) of problems and planned action	Except in emergencies, goals are usually established by means of group participation
Are there forces to accept, resist, or reject goals?	Goals are overtly accepted but are covertly resisted strongly	Goals are overtly accepted but often covertly resisted to at least a moderate degree	Goals are overtly accepted but at times with some covert resistance	Goals are fully accepted both overtly and covertly
7. Character of control processes. Extent to which the review and control functions are concentrated	Highly concentrated in top management	Relatively highly concentrated, with some delegated control to middle and lower levels	Moderate downward delegation of review and control processes; lower as well as higher levels feel responsible	Quite widespread responsibility for review and control, with lower units at times imposing more rigorous reviews and tighter controls than top management

LIKERT'S MANAGEMENT CHARACTERISTICS

Organizational and Performance Characteristics of Different Management Systems Based on a Comparative Analysis

Figure 5.3 (Continued)

	System of organization			
	Authoritative		Consultative System 3	Participative
Organizational variable	Exploitative authoritative System 1	Benevolent authoritative System 2	Consultative System 3	Participative group System 4
Extent to which there is an informal organization present and supporting or opposing goals of formal organization	Informal organization present and opposing goals of formal organization	Informal organization usually present and partially resisting goals	Informal organization may be present and may either support or partially resist goals of formal organization	Informal and formal organization are one and the same; hence all social forces support efforts to achieve organization's goals
Extent to which control data (e.g., accounting, productivity, cost, etc.) are used for self-guidance or group problem solving by managers and non-supervisory employees; or used by superiors in a punitive, policing manner	Used for policing and in punitive manner	Used for policing coupled with reward and punishment, sometimes punitively; used somewhat for guidance but in accord with orders	Largely used for policing with emphasis usually on reward but with some punishment; used for guidance in accord with orders; some use also for self-guidance	Used for self-guidance and for coordinated problem solving and guidance, not used punitively

EXERCISE — PROFILING USING LIKERT'S
MANAGEMENT CHARACTERISTICS

1. Using Likert's Management Characteristics, rank your manager's management style. Turn to Figure 5.3. Beginning with the first column, "Organizational variable," read each description under the bold enumerated headings (e.g., 1. Leadership process used, and so on). After reading each description, work your way across by reading the corresponding "System" descriptions and rank your manager accordingly: System 1 (Exploitative authoritative), or System 2 (Benevolent authoritative), etc.

2. Using the same directions for Step 1 above, complete the exercise for an individual who reports to you.

3. Do the same exercise for yourself.

4. Using the Likert's descriptions under "Participative group — System 4" as the criteria, identify the characteristics where you need improvement.

PART IV. EMPLOYEE NEEDS AND
OBSTACLES TO ACHIEVING THEM

CONTENTS:

Readings — Hierarchy of Human Needs and Motivation

Factors for Each Echelon

Hierarchy Elements for Group Needs

Exercises — Satisfying Employee Egos or Self-Actualization Needs

Obstacles That Prevent Effective Involvement of Employees

READING — HIERARCHY OF HUMAN NEEDS AND MOTIVATION

Physiological and Safety

• Not real motivators; absence caused motivation loss

• Basic "attitude" factors

• Cause dissatisfaction or absence of dissatisfaction

Social

• Minimal real motivators

• Sought in addition to "floor"

Ego

• Ascending motivators

• Some are common to all skill levels

• Loss is powerful dissatisfier

• Generally permanent motivators

Self-Actualization

• Highest motivator

• Most applicable to higher skill levels

• Most permanent motivators

READING — FACTORS FOR EACH ECHELON

Physiological Factors	Safety Factors	Social Factors
Adequate pay for:	Job security	Caliber of associates
Food	Peace of mind	Group relations
Shelter	Supervisory practices	Knowledge of group
Recreation	Maintaining status quo	goals
Rest	Seniority rights	Job status
Physical comforts:		Enjoyment of work
On the job		Social interaction
At home		

Ego Factors

Self-Actualization Factors

Ego Factors	Self-Actualization Factors
Reputation	Realization of individual potential
Self-respect	Liberation of creativity
Competence	New and intense job challenges
Growth	Widest use of aptitude and ability
Achievement	Personal fulfillment
Earned recognition	Maximum self-confidence
Challenging work	
Responsibility	

READING — HIERARCHY ELEMENTS FOR GROUP NEEDS

Social	Esteem	Group Actualization
Acceptance as a group	Recognition	Involvement
Group relations	Group goals	Commitment
Group status	Responsibility	Potential
Group interaction	Achievement	Creativity
	Growth	Challenge
	Team spirit	

EXERCISE — SATISFYING EMPLOYEE EGOS
OR SELF-ACTUALIZATION NEEDS

Fulfilling an individual's ego or self-actualization needs provide greatest motivation.

1. List ten ideas applicable to your company that would provide greatest motivation to employees. Emphasize long-range impact.

2. Beside each idea, indicate whether the cost to attain it would be small or large. Comment on benefits gained versus cost.

3. Discuss and compare with your group.

EXERCISE — OBSTACLES THAT PREVENT EFFECTIVE INVOLVEMENT OF EMPLOYEES

In the average company there are many inherent obstacles preventing an employee from becoming more effectively involved in applying his experience and talent to improve products, services and systems of production or for providing services: It may have to do with the philosophy of the company, i.e., make money fast and then get out. It may have to do with organization where organizational barriers prevent working with others to solve joint problems. It may be written instructions that are confusing or misapplied. Management creates the obstacles and only management can correct them.

1. List ten examples of specific obstacles that prevent effective involvement of employees in your company.

2. Discuss and compare with your group.

PART V. ACHIEVING CONSENSUS AND MAKING DECISIONS

CONTENTS:

Readings — A Conventional Decision-Making Process

   A Consensus Approach

   The Japanese Team Approach

Exercises — A Participative Approach to Achieving a Decision for Change

   Activity A. QC Purchasing System for Suppliers

   Activity B. Inspection System

READING — A CONVENTIONAL DECISION-MAKING PROCESS

There are five steps in the problem-solving and decision-making process: (1) defining the problem, (2) analyzing the problem, (3) developing alternative solutions, (4) deciding on the best solution, and (5) converting the decision into effective action.

The first step, defining the problem, is the crucial step and usually the most difficult one. The problem itself may be part of a larger one, or it may comprise several smaller ones. Some indications of what the problem is may be false and misleading. The use of the scientific method is highly important at this stage.

Steps 2 and 3, analyzing the problem and developing alternative solutions, are relatively easy and usually involve staff work, related research, and such techniques as brainstorming and role playing. The last two steps should flow directly from earlier work. All five steps are described by implication in the following checklist.

Step 1. *Defining the problem:*
Have all relevant facts concerning the problem been collected by using the steps outlined in the scientific method? For example, has the problem been observed first hand? Has information been derived from primary rather than secondary sources?

Has the initial problem definition been revised as more relevant information has become available and irrelevant information discarded?

Has the revised problem definition been submitted to persons who have direct knowledge of the problem situation? Has it met with their satisfaction? Or is there still doubt, confusion, or disagreement about the definition?

Step 2. *Analyzing the problem:*
Has the overall problem been broken down into component parts or subproblems? Has each subproblem been defined?

Has the problem been submitted to study and experimentation in accordance with the principles of the scientific method?

Has the problem solver solicited the views of differing authorities and sources of knowledge?

Which parties have vested interests in the outcome and why? What stakes have they in the outcome?

Are the problem solvers and decision makers the same group or different groups? What inherent or potential conflicts are there between them? What are their vested interests?

Step 3. *Developing alternative solutions:*
Have strawman solutions been formulated to test the understanding of the problem solvers?

Have key variables associated with each selected alternative solution been weighted as to time, cost, benefits, and penalty for a wrong solution?

Have brainstorming, role playing, and other useful techniques been considered at this step?

Step 4. *Deciding on the best solution:*
Has the apparent preferred solution been pilot-tested in the real world, or has it been distilled from laboratory research and analysis?

Have the decision makers tested the problem solvers during this step to insure that both their knowledge and understanding and their technique and methodology are in accordance with prescribed standards and prior agreements and arrangements?

If the preferred solutions turn on only one crucial variable, has the decision maker taken into account the risk and uncertainty element associated with that variable? For example, is a successful outcome too dependent on the materialization of some extremely uncertain event?

Step 5. *Converting the decision into effective action:*
Has a plan that clearly identifies each required action, responsible individual, schedule, and other particulars needed to insure that the decision produces effective action been developed?
What system for monitoring results has been devised?
Is provision made for feedback to insure that actual results can be compared with expected results?
Has a single, responsible person been designated to coordinate the carrying out of the decision? Does that person realize his accountability for implementation and/or results?

READING — A CONSENSUS APPROACH

Decision making by consensus usually yields more creative decisions and more effective implementation than does individual decision making.

Typically, a small group of less than a dozen people will gather, discuss the issue and suggest options. Many meetings are usually required. The need for interpersonal skills in the conduct of these meetings is obvious. A consensus is considered achieved when each individual can honestly say:

I believe that you understand my point of view.

I believe that I understand your point of view.

Whether or not I prefer this decision, I will support it, because it was arrived at in an open and fair manner.

READING — THE JAPANESE TEAM APPROACH

When an important decision needs to be made in a Japanese organization, everyone who will feel its impact is involved in making it. For major decisions as many as 60 or 70 people may be directly involved in making the decision. Teams are assigned to inform all the parties involved. As modifications are made, the teams inform the participants. Many ways are found to brief all the people. Eventually consensus is achieved prior to formalizing the final decision. This process takes a very long time but once a decision is reached, everyone affected by it will be likely to support it.

Though the approach may be a little overdone, there are some valuable concepts. For example:

Time taken beforehand to achieve consensus of those who must implement the decision will probably be less than the time expended persuading the implementers to implement.

The quality of the work of the implementation will be better if they are early participators in the decision-making process.

More knowledge, and possibly critical knowledge, about the forthcoming decision will be revealed prior to formulating the decision.

EXERCISES — A PARTICIPATIVE APPROACH TO ACHIEVING A DECISION FOR CHANGE

Activity A. QC Purchasing System for Suppliers

You believe the system for selecting suppliers, the usual contract provisions about data the supplier should submit, the supplier's accountability for rework revealed at your company's plant and other business relationships can be changed to provide higher quality incoming material at less cost. You are the leader of a decision-making process about whether to commit a major study to investigate feasibility to make such changes. You are told to apply the concept of a participative approach to decision making similar to that used in Japan but not to get lost in a forest of detail.

1. List the titles of the managers, supervisors and key people in your company who might be affected.

2. Which of these individuals will likely have to implement the change?

3. Organize a diagnostic team that would conduct the study.

4. What is your strategy for informing others and achieving consensus?

5. Discuss and compare with your group.

Activity B. Inspection System

You believe the total inspection system from incoming material to delivery to customer requires evaluation and changes to provide better quality at lower cost. For example:

- To substitute more statistical controls for inspectors.

- To rely more on trust and self-control, thereby reducing inspectors.

- To use quality control engineers and inspectors in more effective functions.

- To increase attention to long lead items and humdingers like hi-tech and state-of-the-art components.

- To provide better routines for rinkeydinks.

1. List the titles of the managers, supervisors and key people in your company who might be affected.

2. Which of these individuals will likely have to implement the changes?

3. Organize a diagnostic team that would conduct the evaluation.

4. What is your strategy for informing others and achieving consensus?

5. Discuss and compare with your group.

PART VI. GOAL SETTING

CONTENTS:

READING — CRITERIA FOR EFFECTIVE GOAL SETTING: THE SPIRO MODEL

Personal goals and achievement goals in business are more useful and effective if they are made explicit rather than remaining implicit in one's behavior. Thinking which is purposive is more effective than thinking which is random, jerky, or disjointed. Goal directed behavior is more efficient and more effective than the behavior which is completely spontaneous, unplanned, and disorganized. The alternative to being goal directed is to drift, to float, to achieve in a random manner. Establishing goals explicitly has a great deal of utility. For one thing, planning the next step is much easier if goals are explicit. The management of personal, social, intellectual, and economic development is easier if goals are attainable and have some directional quality to them. Having explicit goals also helps a person in developing a sense of accomplishment. Another benefit to objective goal setting is that a person is far more likely to inventory the resources available to him and to utilize those resources, if his goals are clear. That is not to say that there is no room for serendipity and spontaneity in one's development. In fact, some of the most significant achievements have been made by people who were working toward goals and discovered side effects or observed phenomena that they were not looking for.

The purpose of this exercise is to provide some criteria for judging or critiquing statements of personal goals. Five criteria will be discussed. These five criteria, taken together, constitute the SPIRO model. The five criteria are *specificity, performance, involvement, realism* and *observability.* Applying these five criteria to personal goals can result in more effective goal-setting and more efficient planning.

The first criterion is *specificity.* General goals are less useful than specific ones because the specific ones imply next steps or imply behaviors that need to be changed. An example of a nonspecific goal would be, to improve my sales record next year. An example of a specific goal statement would be, to produce five percent more sales volume on product "X" by the end of the first quarter.

The second criterion is *performance.* "What will I be doing?" Performance-oriented goal statements are more effective in guiding what the person is going to do rather than some nonperformance statements. An example of a non-performance goal would be to increase the productivity level of my subordinates next year. An example of a performance goal might be to develop an action plan this month to resolve each subordinate's job performance situation.

The third criterion is *involvement;* that is, the extent to which the person himself is involved in the objective. An example of a non-involving goal might be to request each subordinate to develop and set their goals. An example of a goal that meets the criterion of involvement might be to meet with each subordinate to mutually set performance goals.

The fourth criterion of effective goal setting is *realism;* that is, the attainability of the goal. An example of an unrealistic goal might be to change the attitudes of the managers to accepting minority group employees. An example of a realistic goal related to that concern might be to acquaint managers with the training opportunities to upgrade the skills of minority job candidates.

The fifth criterion in the SPIRO model is *observability.* This has to do with whether other people can see the result, whether it is obvious that the criterion has been met, or whether the results are overt. An example of a non-observable goal might be to build more self-confidence. A corresponding goal that meets the standard of observability might be to seek out and perform visible group leadership activities.

Applying these five criteria to one's own personal goals and business goals should result in greater understanding of where one is going. It helps if one's goals are made public, if one confides them to another person or publishes them in some way. To commit oneself publicly to growth goals is a way of using one's environment for support to try new behaviors. It is also helpful if goals are time bound; that is, if there are some deadlines involved in the attainment of the objectives. It also helps if one's goals are planned in such a way that there is a good likelihood that there will be some reward from the environment for trying the attainment of that goal.

One idea related to goal setting is contracting. One may write his personal goals, critique them himself, critique them with the help of another person, and develop a contract with the other person that by a certain time he will have accomplished his goal or a certain consequence will take place. For example, an engineer may contract with his wife that he will get a journal article written in the next six months, and if he does not, she will mail his personal check for $50 to the Ku Klux Klan. This is one type of avoidance training.

EXERCISE — INDIVIDUAL AND MANAGERIAL GOALS

(20 min.) 1. Take a few minutes to write your everyday on-the-job goals, critiquing them against these criteria, pairing off with a partner to critique each other's goals, and rewriting goals as necessary in terms of the SPIRO criteria.

(20 min.) 2. Select one of these on-the-job goals that is connected to one of your manager's goals for the organization and discuss with your partner how the achievement of this goal can help your manager better achieve his overall goal so as to produce a "win-win" solution.

"New Basic" — Development and application of manager's skills to improve environments, management style, and attitudes to enable more effective involvement and management of employees.

CHAPTER 6
THE SUPERVISOR'S TRAINING PROGRAM

Supervisors want to participate in training programs when they see interest and involvement by top and line managers. This key to successful supervisor training was demonstrated early by both Texas Instruments and North American Aviation. Companies who profited from that experience have enjoyed enthusiastic and effective participation from their own supervisors. In companies where the establishment of such training programs was delegated to lower echelons of management or farmed out to a consulting firm, supervisor participation has been lethargic.

Inclusion of supervisors in the Management Workshop clearly indicates top and line management interest and involvement. The supervisor takes many of the same sessions as upper, middle and front-line managers. This shows that management recognizes the vital link the supervisor plays in the company and that he is a part of the management team. Supervisors should be scheduled to attend sessions intermingled with front-line managers.

Prerequisite reading for managers who attend the Management Workshop is included in Chapter 3, "Selected American and Japanese Concepts for Developing Environments and Motivating Employees." Greater understanding and significance can be passed on to supervisors if this reading is supplemented with presentations by representatives of upper and middle management. One recommendation is that a member of the top official's steering arm make an initial presentation to specifically welcome the supervisors, cover the purpose of the workshop, and explain the new company philosophy and objectives, emphasizing the attention that both company interests and employee interests will receive. One or more designated middle manager may want to discuss the concepts and tailor them to conditions within the company. Discussion and questions from supervisors should be encouraged.

A supervisor needs to understand and apply the three basics: Empathy, Self-esteem, and Rewards. He must also acquire the skills and techniques to improve the elements of the environment and motivate employees. These include trust, openness, self-control, supervisory characteristics, improving attitudes, and conducting shared goal setting with hourly employees. The supervisor has less need to understand and apply "Implementing Change" and "Consensus and Decision Making." These two sessions have been substituted with "Improving Supportive Relationships Between Managers, Supervisors, and Hourly Employees" and "Improving Hourly Employee Effectiveness," which appear later in this chapter.

The sessions that substitute for "Implementing Change" and "Consensus and Decision Making" concern basic skills and techniques vital to the supervisor's unique position in a company. He is truly the link between those who plan the work and the systems to do it and those who do the work. The supervisor must get the work done—either aided by a desirable environment, or despite an undesirable environment, over which he has limited control. He must get the work done using means for hourly employee involvement provided by management, or despite the obstacles created by management—over which he has limited control. Often the supervisor must get the work done using the best way—not necessarily the way described by confusing or misapplied written instructions—and then protect the workers for not following procedures. These negative conditions may not have been created by management to prevent attaining better quality and productivity nor to create some adversarial relations between employees, supervisors and managers. But they often do.

Managers must take the first step to improve the linkage. The Supervisor's Training Program is such a step, but it requires effort by all three parties, management, supervisors and employees. The result can be a mutually supportive environment with substantial increase in quality and productivity of services, systems and products. By the time supervisors begin their training, most managers will be acquainted with top management's commitment to improving the company environment. The introduction by a member of the steering arm and middle managers' presentations about concepts should condition supervisors to the idea that management is responsive to upward communication. Following the training, it is largely up to supervisors to inform and influence hourly employees to the many changes taking place. Both managers and supervisors must overcome what amounts to a social change in relations in many companies—particularly larger corporations. In many companies there still exist traditional lines of distinction between management and professional employees vs. supervisors and hourly employees. Because of this, supervisors often have an instinctive desire for low visibility and minimum interference from management and professional employees. Managers often use supervisors as the excuse for not making more frequent visits to the shop floor or other hourly employee work areas. This is particularly true for many front-line managers with little experience in the world of the hourly employee. These conditions exist to a lesser degree with companies in Japan and other trade deficit companies primarily because there are fewer echelons of management in these companies.

When the negative relationships are viewed as part of the business enterprise, these customary distinctions become examples of how management can shoot itself in the foot. The Japanese concepts of trust, subtlety and intimacy, briefly described in this book, come into play. So do the other concepts of American and Japanese origin described in Chapter 3. The sessions attended by supervisors and front-line managers are planned to change these negative distinctions. The first substitute session is targeted to upward and downward communication. The second substitute session deals with relations between supervisors and hourly employees.

The first substitute session is "Improving Supportive Relations Between Managers, Supervisors and Hourly Employees." The session teaches ways to improve relations and emphasizes the need for follow-up and on-the-job training. The session includes improving trust and communication upwards and downwards and is to be attended by front-line managers as well as supervisors.

The second substitute session is concerned with relations between supervisors and hourly employees. Its focus is on how the supervisor can attain more effective involvement by his or her employees.

It is common practice for a manager to thoroughly indoctrinate a new professional employee in his job. They have a written position description to help explain the individual's job, which includes written performance factors that will be used to evaluate the individual's performance. The individual is introduced to his manager and to all professional associates with whom he will have dealings. Arrangements are made to brief the employee about the company and the work of his own and related organizations. Annually he will receive a written and oral appraisal of his performance. Guidance is included on improving performance as needed along with career guidance. The employee is usually given opportunity to continue his education to further his career, at company expense. In due time he becomes eligible for more and more perks and finally executive compensation or other added incentive compensation. The result is usually a well-educated and highly productive professional employee who has been motivated and rewarded.

An overview of the situation for the supervisor and the hourly employee reveals that commensurate practices do not exist in most companies. The cost to apply commensurate practices is negligible when compared to the increase in quality and productivity of products, services and systems that can be expected as a result. Experts' lists of obstacles to more effective involvement of hourly employees are filled with failures to apply these commensurate practices. The lists contain such examples as: "What is my job?", "How do I know if I am performing it satisfactorily?", "Why doesn't my supervisor or the manager ask me my views for improving the product, making procedures more usable, and how to cut costs?", "Where am I going to be ten years from now?", etc. It is only human nature—and a means to acquire self-esteem and esteem from others—to want to contribute one's experience and knowledge to improve products, services and systems. The second substitute session, "Improving the Effectiveness of Hourly Employees," includes follow-up and on-the-job training.

The Supervisor's Training Program also includes a separate course in analytical and statistical methods. In American schools and industry, it has been customary to restrict such training to professional and technical employees. In Japan, supervisors and hourly employees are given this training as a major tool to increase their effectiveness. Dr. Kaoru Ishikawa includes excellent material for this training in his book *Guide to Quality Control*. There is no reasonable basis for the restriction in America. Most supervisors and hourly employees are high school graduates or have attended trade schools. They have sufficient prerequisites to complete such a course.

PART I. IMPROVING SUPPORTIVE RELATIONSHIPS BETWEEN MANAGERS, SUPERVISORS, AND HOURLY EMPLOYEES

CONTENTS:

READING —
"A STEELWORKER TALKS MOTIVATION"
BY DONALD T. DALENA

THE U.S. SYSTEM of management hasn't gone awry. The assumption that something suddenly has "gone wrong" is fallacious because of a presumption that the system was "right" at one time or another. But it wasn't.

My thesis rests upon a simple premise and a basic conclusion: A company has two broad types of resources at its disposal: *property resources* (machinery, equipment, raw materials, and buildings) and *human resources* (the talent, both physical and mental, of all engaged in productive activity). The emphasis has been placed on the former, while the human potential has been largely untapped.

Emphasis is finally being placed on dealing with worker alienation and dissatisfaction because:

• Their cost can no longer be freely passed on to consumers.

• A better educated and better informed workforce is far less tolerant of intrinsic work conditions than were our predecessors.

Bluecollar worker: an 'in' topic

Writing about the bluecollar worker and diagnosing his ills are definitely "in." A parade of eminent psychologists, journalists, and commentators is expounding on the deadly effects of "barren boredom."

All sorts of quack cures have been prescribed, ranging from art on the assembly line to less spare time for workers. Chuckleheaded ideas abound, one of the more frightening being the suggestion that workers plan and control their work even to the point of encroaching on management decision making.

New terms bordering on misnomers are part of the "in" language. Who hasn't heard of the "bluecollar blues" and "job enrichment"? The movement is rank with motivation studies and a fantastic assembly-line hang-up wherein most bluecollar workers are depicted as robots tied to a production line.

There's even a counterculture claiming that motivation is the worker's worry, not management's; that the worker's right to bitch about the job, the boss, and the system is an "inalienable right"; and that unions must have been thinking of job enrichment when they negotiated certain benefits. Ad infinitum and ad nauseam.

Advocates of a richer worklife crawling out of the woodwork include the U.S. government, which authorized what may be the greatest piece of ivory-tower literature of our time, a 211-page report titled *Work in America.*

Popular prescriptions not the cure

Is job enrichment needed? Are bluecollar jobs demeaning and deadly? Should we fit the job to the worker? Will putting our names on a product instill pride? Shall boredom be attacked by having workers assemble the entire unit rather than handle it in part? Does the answer lie in allowing us to do more than our job descriptions allow? Should we boss ourselves and be allowed to "weed out" those with whom we cannot work?

Baloney!

Envision a car going down the road burdened with an enormous plaque bearing an endless list of all the workers who contributed to its creation, ranging from those who mined the ore to the name of the final quality control inspector. Imagine the grievances over whose name gets on what product.

We American workers are the most productive in the world. We can outthink, outproduce, and outfight our counterparts throughout the world, as history indeed shows, but only when the desire is there. And the desire could easily be instilled because we want it instilled.

In order to do so, equal emphasis must be placed on the human side of productivity, a side thus far ignored in our near-psychotic quest for machine or technological productivity. Our entire system of management is geared toward alienation, but it doesn't have to be. The change can be easy, painless, and uncomplicated.

The truth is that most jobs can't be enriched but the lives of workers sure can be. I see things differently from the others, perhaps because I earn my living as a factory worker in a steel mill. I see no complex problem nor suggest a formula-type solution.

Three simple keys are necessary to unlock the door to human progress within the workplace: *care, continuous feedback,* and *the feeling of mutual need.*

Care: almost too easy

Industrial managers must care more than a little about workers. Care is a mirror, its output accurately reflecting the input. Managers who manifest care will eliminate stress, promote trust, and improve attitude and morale.

How? It's almost too easy.

The work shift actually begins when workers arrive on or near plant property. Traffic flow, and better, closer, and more secure parking are musts. Managers who don't provide them are ignorant and wasteful. Care begins by assuring that workers arrive in a frame of mind that is conducive to work.

Visible, archaic signs of a violent past continue to haunt us. Daily we see plant guards wearing sidearms, needlessly creating a quasiprison atmosphere. We know why guns *were* worn, but why *are* they? Untrusted, we must present an identification badge in order to gain entry to work for the company to which we've committed our work lives.

Equally important is that tools, materials, and equipment are readily available to enable the job to be done with as little aggravation as possible.

Managers err in waiting until the union makes requests for improvement at local negotiations. A union-won benefit does not have the same effect as one which is freely given because its need was recognized and because company officials care.

The feeling—the tangible knowledge—that someone cares is a necessary one in order for us to freely give our best. Often when the feeling of care exists, just striving for improvement—even if it fails—will have the same effect as an implemented improvement.

'They don't give a damn'

I can vividly remember bringing what I believed to be both a problem and an element of frustration to the attention of a railroad inspector who visited my work area. (Part of my job consists of loading and securing tin plate coils and bundles in boxcars for shipment to customers.)

The problem, I explained, was that the cross-members provided us to secure the loads were about a half-inch too short, and I asked if he would please do something about this.

Snobbishly, he looked at me through unprotected eyes at my sweat-steamed safety goggles and asked, "What do you do about it? Obviously you're loading and not rejecting the cars."

I enlightened him with, "We take that big tractor over there and hump the cars on each side until they're bowed in."

His solution was typical of what we encounter. "Well, keep humping them." I felt like humping *him* with the tractor. The company manager accompanying him smiled and said nothing. I recall thinking, "They don't give a damn. Why should we?"

In our minds are locked solutions, answers, and clues to answers of everyday problems. Why not consult us? A prime example of what could be done is in consulting us prior to ordering new mobile equipment.

Mobile equipment is ordered primarily by specification. We don't see it until it's literally tossed at us to operate. Consequently, we're often stuck with equipment that jars our bodies, decreases the sensitivity of our hearing, and upsets us in countless other ways.

We have two forklift tractors in our department which are fast and can carry heavy loads—but that's all. I'd love to have the dollars in damage these tractors cause each year because we can't see the product we're picking up. Aggravations from poor design include being nudged by an improperly located battery connector, tramping on the brake only to have the brake pedal depress on your other foot, having three separate control levers when one could be made to perform all three functions, and having a tractor everyone hates because it's nearly impossible to change the batteries. These do little to demonstrate to us that someone cares.

These tell us, instead, that someone doesn't give a damn about us. Each time we use such ill-designed equipment, it's like receiving a brand-new slap across the face; it's insulting, agitating, and contributes a negative effect.

Care can be shown in countless other ways. Each manager can find his own list of examples should he care to.

Neither a kick nor a pat on the back

Feedback is the second key. Feedback for workers usually consists of receiving a good chewing out or a discipline slip because an order or job was messed up. To worsen matters, there are times when this particular class of feedback comes from the wrong manager in the form of interference.

Do we want a pat on the back? No. That isn't feedback, although an occasional word of acknowledgment properly placed won't hurt.

Rather, we want to know our competitive standing with our customers, where the product has come from, what happens to it after it leaves us, its planned future use, and current problems connected with its production which influence our work lives in one form or another.

Company, workers need each other

Care and feedback are important elements but not *the* important one. The main ingredient lacking in the workplace is the feeling of mutual need. Were it present, care and feedback would be natural effects. It's the one element that's overlooked by psychologists, consultants, and professional writers.

Top managers have not allowed a simple fact to speak to them: Each worker is there because he wants to work. He came for a job. He needs the company. The worker, therefore, has made a commitment to that company.

But there is no reciprocity. If the company's managers reacted equally—by recognizing that they hired a worker for a job because they need a worker for the job—and based their supervisory philosophy accordingly, many, many problems would vanish. The worker is there because he is needed. Companies don't do workers a favor by hiring them any more than workers do the company a favor by choosing them to work for. Yet this fact is constantly ignored.

Lacking this balanced outlook, a natural effect of the present system is poor quality of supervision. The supervisor is there to supervise, not to browbeat and intimidate. Supervisors with sandpaper personalities just don't belong in today's workplace. They should be retrained, reassigned, or retired. Before we can feel ourselves a needed part of a team, our supervisors must feel it first. Theirs is the example to set. But first their proper roles must be assumed.

To his men, a front-line foreman should be a leader, not someone to fight with or kowtow to. We relate to the foreman and he to us. We're a part of each other, or should be. His crew is his responsibility. His should be the recognized right to fight and fight hard for his own when he believes a wrong has befallen them. Fight for his men? A foreman? Hah! Woe betide the foreman who argues on behalf of one or all of his men.

The same goes for the middle and upper-middle manager. Each has certain responsibilities which should not interfere with the others'. The input we receive at the grassroots is a lack of delegated responsibility down the management ladder and encroachment on the rights of lower supervisors. Often this results in a lack of responsibility—even in irresponsibility—at the worker level.

Each manager should encourage, rather than discourage and interfere with the role of the other. I've seen managers practically live in the plant, but exhibit little or no regard for the rights of subordinates. As a result, all that time spent is in vain, their presence causing more harm than benefit.

To us, top managers are objects of fear and scorn instead of the pillars of respect they ought to be and that we'd like them to be. They're people we're visibly better off without, we figure. Necessary, yes, but invisible. All of us have experienced the results of their nit-picking tours: upsetting our all too delicate worker-foreman relationships. To them, a worker holding a cup of coffee is an open affront, not someone taking a needed break. The poor foreman is chewed out because his men are standing around. We feel like unwanted baggage.

The lack of recognition of mutual need has necessitated the continuance of supervision by fear and punishment, a condition that cannot lead to encouraging and enabling each worker to achieve his full potential.

This is an antiquated method transplanted by the colonizers from England and Europe. We're expected to produce in a sort of perpetual debtor's prison as indentured servants. It's an ingrained idea that must be sanded out of our system if we're looking for other than technological advance.

Creation of self-actualized man

Once we workers feel and know we are needed and wanted, that someone cares, that we are an important part of something because we are important, that our work talent and productive minds are desired, then our labor will be a labor of love.

The most boring jobs, the most grueling physically taxing jobs, the most menial jobs would be pleasureful tasks leading to fulfillment of individual sense of worth.

Only then can we cease being *economic man* motivated solely by economic forces, cease being *frightened man* motivated by fear of what will happen if we don't produce as expected, and become *self-actualized man* motivated by desire.

Certainly there will always be those malcontents and recalcitrants whom we undoubtedly would be better off without. But the feeling and the knowledge of mutual need will challenge us to utilize their productive minds, encouraging them to live with us as we live with them.

To expect a sterile in-plant society is as unrealistic a goal as attempting to create an aseptic community. Yet this goal is constantly and mistakenly pursued by industry. Each firing, however justified, creates fear. Each exercise of discipline effects intimidation.

Progress will come in small steps

Results can't be achieved overnight. First and foremost there must be the desire to tap the human potential. Next is a continuing series of small steps.

My advice to managers is to think small. Look for those seemingly infinitesimal and picayune frustrations that cumulatively produce stress and anxiety. Ferret them out and correct them. Stop fighting boredom; fight frustration. Treat the job-holder meaningfully. Treat him as a person whose needs command as much attention as the machine he operates.

Stop worrying about how long the worker's hair is and worry about him instead. Stop treating injured workers as if they wanted to be injured. Listen to those gripes. Workers are trying to tell you to find a different way, a better way to do the job.

Fortunately, the problem is receiving some top-level attention of sorts. Hopeful signs are emerging that there is a recognition that we need and should help each other. The major sign is the new Experimental Negotiating Agreement reached between the nation's major steel producers and my own union, the United Steelworkers of America.

If this feeling of mutual need filters down to the workplace then our work lives (instead of our jobs) will be enriched.

But there's still a great deal to be overcome. Through our unions, we've had to fight for everything we have. Mistrust has been and remains our blood brother. We've been given only what we've won, and sometimes not even that. Why then should we give more than we're required to give?

Adversity has been a natural effect. All this can be changed because the time is ripe for a change and because change is needed and desired.

Work in America was wrong in calling U.S. bluecollar workers "forgotten people"; we're merely neglected people, our potential talents remaining dormant and untapped.

Can U.S. industry afford to continue this waste?

(This article originally appeared in *Industry Week*, January 14, 1974, pp. 26-30. Reprinting of this article has been granted with the express permission of the author, Donald T. Dalena.)

READING —
" 'SOMETHING IS OUT OF WHACK'
IN U.S. BUSINESS MANAGEMENT" —
A Conversation with Tom Peters

"Everybody talks quality"—it's mostly lip service

American business management is in a state of thoughtful turmoil. It's not out of the doldrums in any sense. The old rust-bowl industries aren't yet within a million miles of being competitive. Everybody talks quality, but most of that is lip service. I'm not terribly sanguine about the prospects of big business becoming very vital from an entrepreneurial standpoint. And the staffs of the Fortune 500 companies are still hopelessly bloated despite cuts of 40 to 50 percent.

Yet I find it heartening that there is now zero complacency. When we talk about the U.S. economy, we're talking about a giant beast, and to simply wake that beast up, as has happened in the last half-dozen years, is a gigantic accomplishment. That's a vast change from the years between 1946 and 1973—the boom period ended by the OPEC crisis—when management was thought to be reasonably infallible. So there's lots of motion, lots of searching, lots of anguish and still too much of a tendency to look to government for solutions as opposed to looking to the work force.

Employees: "Part of the solution," not the problem

The major failure of American business is seeing the employee as part of the problem instead of as part of the solution. If you track the language carefully in Fortune 100 chief-executive-officer speeches, you still pick up automation rather than retraining and redeployment of the work force as the salvation of business. I saw a 21-page summary of interesting things going on at General Motors, and the first mention of people didn't come until page 20.

Another shortcoming is that Americans are really poor internationalists. We don't speak other people's languages, an indicator that we don't take the international world very seriously. The argument that English is the language of commerce is just a bunch of junk as far as I'm concerned. I grant that the playing field internationally is not level in the case of such countries as Japan. But while the average American manager would blame 85 percent of the problem on external forces, my hypothesis is that only half of the problem is external and the rest is internal, self-imposed by management. And our business schools certainly don't focus on international management skills.

Still, from the Cokes to the Gillettes to the IBM's, there are examples of superb international management in the U.S. economy, even relative to the Japanese. Most of these companies are willing to take an incredibly long period of time to develop relationships in foreign markets—they sometimes live without profit a dozen years—and they have a fairly high dose of internationals in senior-management ranks.

"An excess of 'the administrative mentality' "

American management suffers from an excess of "the administrative mentality." During and after World War II, many large enterprises became managed by administrator-finance sorts of people. Business schools then started to produce more such people; faculties became populated increasingly by those people. Courses on manufacturing and selling dropped way down and were replaced principally by courses in finance, accounting and decision science. Now, if you will, both sides of the coin are rotten: The M.B.A.-producing mechanism and what you find in the senior-executive suites of an awful lot of companies.

You look at the backgrounds of managers who have come up through the ranks and you find an incredibly low share of people who spent the majority of their career designing, making, selling and servicing, even though business is fundamentally about just those things. Something is out of whack.

Growing up with a "dose of reality" helps

I have this feeling, which may be the most hopeless naïveté in the world, that if managers spent some part of their formative years on a production line or in the sales branch in Podunk trying to peddle 80-jillion-dollar machinery to people who have a salary of $3.95 an hour, they'd never view life the same way. If they grew up with that dose of reality, they probably wouldn't slip so far after they entered executive positions.

But what we do is hammer into the heads of business people that they should aspire to be "professional managers." And what is the definition of a professional manager? A person who doesn't get involved in the micro-details. That means: "Keep your tail in the office." I run into perfectly intelligent human beings who feel funny when they're out of the office; it's as if they're doing something wrong.

You get into these monsters called the Fortune 500 companies where managers have surrounded themselves with unbelievably brilliant, thoughtful, attractive staff people who give them unbelievably brilliant, thoughtful analyses. That makes them feel they're doing the right thing by sitting there.

A very different model—one that does things the right way—is the Trammel Crow real-estate organization, which recruits heavily in the highly rated business schools. Without exception, the Stanford M.B.A. who comes to that company will spend the first three years of his or her career peddling low-price warehouse space in the East Los Angeleses of the world. That's great because if the M.B.A. is worth a damn, then that person will survive those three years, learn a lot of humility and a lot about the real world; their analytic skills will get blended with that real-world experience. That's my ideal.

"Involved" vs. "bottom line" approaches

What we see when things work well in a company is an unbelievably involved, vigorous, vital—and probably not brilliant—manager who is out talking, testing stuff and listening to anybody he or she can grab hold of. But it's hard to do that with all the distractions that take place in the course of the day and with every force driving managers toward things that look a lot more tangible in terms of their bottom-line impact.

Still, there are executives like Sam Walton, who runs Wal-Mart, a company I happen to dote on. He visits about 750 stores a year. How does he find that time, running a 7-billion-dollar-a-year business, when the retailer next door, who has three stores, can't visit them but once a year? That retailer is distracted by 87,000 legitimate, competing priorities. But Walton says: "See you. I'm off to the stores." How do you get people to bite that particular apple? I don't know. It's the great frustration of my life.

"Nobody asks" workers to suggest improvements

Some of the solutions I offer to problems afflicting management, such as attention to quality and customers, may seem obvious. But time after time when I'm wandering around a plant I talk to somebody who has been employed at the same machine for 12 years. I don't understand the machinery, but I have a 20-minute conversation with them, and they tell me 97 things that could be slightly improved and wouldn't cost more than a few nickels' worth of capital. You say to that person at the end of the talk: "Why don't you tell somebody about it?" You get this unbelievably pathetic answer: "Nobody asked."

A guy who retired a few years ago who ran quality control in a sizable division of a Big Three auto company said that in a dozen years in that job he was never visited by a member of the corporate staff and only once by his division general manager. That says to me that the company didn't care about quality. What can you recommend when that's the case?

(Reprinted from *U.S. News & World Report* issue of July 15, 1985. Copyright, 1985, *U.S. News & World Report*.)

READING — A WAY TO INCREASE TRUST AND COMMUNICATION ACROSS BOUNDARY LINES

Donald Dalena, in his article, "A Steelworker Talks Motivation," told of the need for increased trust and communication between managers, supervisors and hourly employees as it existed a decade ago. "A Conversation with Tom Peters" reveals that the same need exists today. A few of our best managed companies, including Hewlett-Packard, Texas Instruments, the new Saturn complex of General Motors, McDonald's and Dana have recognized that need and executed strong measures to improve upward and downward communication, encourage self-control and create an environment of mutual need and trust. However, the vast majority of companies fail to address the problem.

Little has been written about how to improve the relationships between managers, supervisors and hourly employees. The above companies observed practices in Japan or were innovative in developing their own concepts and methods. Yet, this relationship is a keystone in the emerging industrial revolution that promotes more effective involvement of employees as the means with greatest potential to improve quality and productivity.

Management created the existing relationships that include unnecessary adversarial factors which inhibit quality and productivity. So management must take the first steps to initiate change. The steps must be strong on action, not just on words. Supervisors are the "linking pin" and can make a substantial contribution. The hourly employee can, too, when given the chance. It's a joint venture. Everyone gains.

Back to typical adversarial relations. When things go wrong, it is easy to find reasons to blame someone else. Management looks at hourly employees and blames them for management's inability to compete, i.e., high labor costs. Hourly employees look at management and blame them for being unable to make headway rowing the boat because there are so many excessive echelons of management riding free. Managers, supervisors and hourly employees tend to dwell on such adversarial relations because there do not exist ready means to improve relations.

There are good reasons to believe that a way can be readily found to communicate for the purpose of improving relations. Complaints are seldom personalized. They are usually aimed at a group such as management or hourly employees, another organization within the company, and frequently with the government. There exists respect and esteem for talent between managers and hourly employees. The number of times a supervisor has pulled management out of a hole to meet customer commitment is matched by the amount of business obtained from management to keep the company alive and provide jobs for employees. The most important reason is each of the three parties needs each other and they know it.

So how can we create a way to improve relations? We are acquainted with meetings with useful purposes and we are acquainted with meetings that are worthless. An example of the former is the periodic staff meetings of a line manager with his subordinate managers that achieve downward and upward communications on administrative and work agendas. Another example is periodic Round Tables of supervisors with hourly employees also achieving downward and upward communication on administrative and work agendas. Managers do communicate with supervisors but it is usually one-on-one for the purpose of passing downward information or directions. It is rare that periodic meetings are held between front-line managers, supervisors and occasionally hourly employees as appropriate. It is even more rare that they discuss special accomplishments, obstacles preventing employees from doing work, ideas of employees to improve products, services and systems, and news of the business of interest to employees.

Such meetings have a useful purpose. It is time to start them. In addition, to make the meetings more fruitful, managers need to permit and authorize reasonable amounts of time and freedom for supervisors and hourly employees to refine and develop ideas. Managers can provide the quality circles or authorize activity by an individual.

The exercise that follows helps develop skills and methods for conducting such meetings. It also provides opportunity to acquire cumulative information about obstacles and ideas.

Establishing such meetings company-wide requires time, care and the involvement of top management. Once established, follow-on guidance is needed to iterate improvement and sustain the meetings. Three ways are suggested. One is occasional attendance by a third party, the instructor, who observes and later provides guidance. Another is occasional attendance by a middle manager who observes and later provides guidance. The "skip-manager" technique also is useful here. Occasionally the front-line manager's superior conducts the meeting. This tends to stimulate the meetings and benefits the superior.

EXERCISE — INCREASING TRUST AND
COMMUNICATION ACROSS BOUNDARY LINES

The mixed class of front-line managers and supervisors should subdivide into smaller groups containing a minimum of two managers and two supervisors. The subgroups should prepare for and conduct a mock meeting as described below.

Managers will prepare a list of three recent news items, events or accomplishments pertinent to the business of the company and of interest to enlightened supervisors and hourly employees.

The supervisor will:

* List at least three significant accomplishments of individuals in the group of hourly employees that occurred in the past month.

* List at least three obstacles that, if removed, would permit more effective involvement of hourly employees to improve quality of productivity.

* List at least three ideas learned from hourly employees for improving products, services or systems, and recommend how best to pursue the ideas, i.e., with an existing or new Americanized version of a quality circle, or permitting freedom and allocating resources to an individual.

Each manager will conduct a mock meeting with three or more supervisors. The agenda items and persons responsible are:

Information about the business — the manager

Accomplishments — a supervisor

Obstacles — a supervisor

Ideas — a supervisor

Summing up agreed-upon
obstacles and ideas — the manager

A management spokesman should be selected to summarize the exercise with the total class.

PART II. IMPROVING HOURLY EMPLOYEE EFFECTIVENESS
CONTENTS:

Readings — What is My Job (A Four-Step Instruction)

Sixteen Job Factors for Quality Performance

Basic Quality Performance Requirements

Appraisal Interviewing

Exit Interviews

Exercise — Improving Supervisor and Worker Effectiveness

READING — WHAT IS MY JOB?
A FOUR-STEP INSTRUCTION

Step 1: Prepare the worker.
  Put him at ease.
  State the job and find out what he already knows about it.
  Get him interested in learning the job.
  Place in correct position.
Step 2: Present the operation.
  Tell, show, and illustrate one important step at a time.
  Stress each key point.
  Instruct clearly, completely, and patiently, but no more than he can master.
Step 3: Try out performance.
  Have him do the job—correct errors.
  Have him explain each key point to you as he does the job again.
  Make sure he understands.
  Continue until you know he knows.
Step 4: Follow up.
  Put him on his own. Designate the person to whom he goes for help.
  Check frequently. Encourage questions.
  Taper off extra coaching and close follow-up.

READING — SIXTEEN JOB FACTORS FOR QUALITY PERFORMANCE

The work of Dr. Herzberg gives us some clear insight into ways that supervisors can determine the motivational make-up of a subordinate. Herzberg classifies motives into two categories: "satisfiers," a motive that is appeased by being satisfied; and, "motivators," a motive that is *not* appeased by being satisfied and which takes on increased motivating property through the very process of striving to achieve the goal.

Herzberg used a critical incident method to collect stories from employees about job situations which had been either extremely gratifying or very dissatisfying. Their directions to respondents were as follows: "Think of a time in the past when you felt especially good or bad about your job. It may have been *this* job or any other. Can you think of such a high or low point in your feelings of your job? Please tell me about it." The stories were classified according to job factors which were reflected in them.

Herzberg identifies 16 separate job factors:

1. Achievement—to complete a job successfully or to fail to do a job adequately.

2. Recognition—to be singled out for praise or criticism and blame.

3. Work Itself—to like or to dislike the actual task involved in getting the job done.

4. Responsibility—to gain responsibility for your own or others work or to lack responsibility in a job.

5. Advancement—to change status through promotion or demotion, or to miss an expected promotion.

6. Salary—to obtain a salary increase or to lose out on an expected one.

7. Possibility for Growth—changes in a job which could lead to further growth or which could be stultifying.

8. Interpersonal Relations with Subordinates—to experience either satisfying or dissatisfying attractions with one's subordinates.

9. Status—to obtain some actual sign pertinent to status or to lose it.

10. Interpersonal Relations with Superiors—to experience either satisfying or dissatisfying social attractions with one's boss.

11. Interpersonal Relations with Co-workers—to experience either satisfying or dissatisfying social attractions with one's co-workers.

12. Technical Aspects of Supervision—to have a competent supervisor or to have an incompetent one.

13. Company Policy Administration—to be in a company with good possibilities, policies, and good administrative procedures or to be in one with poor ones.

14. Working Conditions—to have good physical surroundings on the job or to have poor ones.

15. Personal Life—to have one's personal life affected for good or ill by occurrences on the job.

16. Job Security—objective indications of security such as job tenure and company stability.

The results of Herzberg's research are startling. The findings suggest rather clearly that especially satisfying, and therefore potentially motivating, job situations differ from especially dissatisfying job situations. Satisfying situations are characterized by opportunities to experience achievement, recognition, a sense of responsibility, and advancement in jobs which are intrinsically interesting to the respondents. In contrast, the dissatisfying situation most often involves incompetent supervision, poor company policies, administrative criticism, and poor working conditions. Unusually good supervision and good company policies are rarely mentioned in this, describing especially satisfying situations.

Herzberg concludes that certain job factors (supervision, company policies, and working conditions) cannot be utilized to motivate employees. They can at best be expected to prevent negative feelings and dissatisfaction.

READING —
BASIC QUALITY PERFORMANCE REQUIREMENTS

Since the results from quality motivation training should be measured in terms of actual output, it is important to consider the relationship between motivational factors and other factors which influence employee performance. The basic requirements for a program to promote high quality performance are:

- Realistic and clearly defined quality goals.
- Procedure for relating quality goals to individual needs and goals.
- Opportunity for personal responsibility and involvement in establishing individual goals.
- Participation in defining and solving problems which limit product quality.
- Individual measures of quality performance.
- Rapid knowledge of results and evaluation.
- Specific examples of important defects and suggestions for eliminating them.
- Recognition and reward for achieving quality goals.

READING — APPRAISAL INTERVIEWING

An appraisal interview is a *purposeful* conversation between a supervisor and his subordinate. The emphasis here is on the concept of a *purposeful* conversation. A supervisor may carry on a number of conversations during the course of the day with his subordinates, but an interview, to be productive, must be a *purposeful* conversation. There are a variety of purposes for an interview. The supervisor may be seeking information from the subordinate, he may be looking to give information to the subordinate, or he may be interested in correcting the subordinate's performance.

In the case we are talking about, the supervisor is searching for factors that will give him evidence of the employee's motivation. There are four basic steps to conducting a *purposeful* conversation that will determine the motivation of a subordinate.

First, create an appropriate atmosphere. If the conversation is to be successful, it is up to the supervisor to put the employee at ease, to make him feel relaxed, and to let him know that the supervisor really and sincerely wants to know what he has to say. The supervisor does this by smiling, showing interest in personal aspects of the subordinate's job. In the beginning of any purposeful conversation with the employee, the supervisor seeks to establish essential human contact with the subordinate.

Second, establish the purpose of the conversation. Natural suspicion on the part of the subordinate prevents him from discussing frankly with the supervisor the problems the supervisor has in mind. It is essential, once the employee is at ease and an appropriate climate has been established, that the supervisor state explicitly why he is conducting the interview.

Third, ask a leadoff question. This question has to be open, that is, it must start with words like: who, what, when, where, which or how. Open questions start conversations. Many supervisors try to start conversations with questions that begin with: is, do, has, can, or will. These are closed questions and effectively *stop* the flow of conversation.

Fourth, simply listen. Having asked a question or two in the appropriate climate, it is then the responsibility of a good supervisor to *listen* to what the subordinate has to say. A good interviewer should listen at least *60%* of the time and talk only *40%* or less.

In the kind of interview we have in mind here, the main listening technique that a supervisor must use is the pause. During the pause, the supervisor shows interest by direct eye contact and a friendly smile or nod, but does not intrude with any words or further questions.

The next step in an effective interview, after a suitable interval of listening, is to pursue the key ideas a subordinate will introduce in any purposeful conversation. The supervisor refers back to the body of the conversation and asks another question, making reference to the key idea. In this case, the key idea is relating to those motivational factors.

READING — EXIT INTERVIEW

Another type of interview is the exit interview. The purpose behind the exit interview is to determine why the individual is terminating his service. Here we are trying to gain information rather than motivate action. To be successful, the interview should provide a free expression of thought. For this reason, many experts suggest that the exit interview be performed by individuals outside the sphere of relationship of the person terminating. Such circumstances will frequently reveal deficiencies in motivation and human relationships on the job. Information from the exit interview may be used to correct counter-motivation of other employees. It is also an excellent medium for obtaining possible unbiased information for further investigation and thought.

EXERCISE — IMPROVING SUPERVISOR AND WORKER EFFECTIVENESS

The supervisor can improve his management of people and their productivity by applying some of the basic practices given to professional employees but often neglected for hourly employees. These basic practices are included in answers to the following questions which may be voiced by an hourly employee:

1. "What is my job?"
2. "How do I know if I am performing my job satisfactorily?"
3. "What is the function of the organization to which I belong and the function of related organizations?"
4. "With whom will I interface?"

Subdivide the class into groups of six supervisors. All six supervisors are to do the preparation work described below. However, for the mock one-on-one encounters between a supervisor and his hourly employee, a supervisor must be designated to play the part of the hourly employee.

- Each supervisor shall write a brief yet clear and specific description of the job of one of his employees.

- He will also outline the performance factors against which the employee will be appraised.

- The supervisor should list the names and functions of individuals with whom the employee will interface, including the supervisor's manager.

- The function of the organization, as well as related organizations, should also be compiled.

- Each supervisor will next engage in two encounters with the "acting" hourly employee. The purpose of the first encounter is to describe the employee's job and the performance appraisal factors. During the second encounter, the employee's performance is appraised.

CHAPTER 7
TOP MANAGEMENT INVOLVEMENT, LEADERSHIP, AND STRUCTURE: ESSENTIAL ELEMENTS

It may seem elementary to suggest the top official must be behind management involvement. But it is not enough that the top official back the activity — or approve the activity — or support the activity. Top management needs to become involved also and realize the importance of his commitment. He must lead the effort. Employees will observe his leadership, or lack of it, and respond accordingly.

A SEQUENCE FOR CHANGE

Top officials of some of America's most innovative and best-managed companies have evolved successful sequences for effecting change. These officials recognize the need to improve environments and attitudes throughout the company *before* involving employees in ways to improve quality and productivity. They understand that you must know the competence of competitors before you can plan to attain superior competence. They have learned about and experienced "existing" company environments, attitudes, and obstacles to employee involvement before attempting improvements. They also have learned about favorable features, problems, and opportunities to improve products, services, and systems before initiating premature programs to upgrade them.

Although some of the sequences seem obvious, the careful planning of sequence was a major factor for success — neglect to do the obvious was a major reason for failure. An example is America's adoption of quality circles. By 1982, a study by the New York Stock Exchange reported that 44% of all companies with over 500 employees had quality circle programs. It was estimated that over 90% of the Fortune 500 companies had quality circles. Most companies had hurriedly contracted with consultants in essence to copy the Japanese methods. The sequence, described below, to acquire background knowledge, develop manager's skills, create improved environments and attitudes, increase incentives and readiness before involving employees, was skipped. As reported, quality circles in many cases were simply something the "top told the middle to do to the bottom." In 1985, the *Harvard Business Review* reported the unsatisfactory experiences of many companies. The report took us back to square one to reprepare for and readapt the concept of quality circles in forms more applicable to American workers.

The following sequence comes from the *successful* companies. It is interesting to note its close relationship with the "Universal Sequences for Breakthrough Management" developed by Dr. J. M. Juran for the American Management Association.

1. The sequence begins with homework to round out knowledge of why and how we lost our eminent position in quality and productivity, and how our competitors have overtaken us in quality and are about to overtake us in productivity. It is from this understanding that we learn the current competence of competitors, what superior competence we must acquire, and how we can acquire it.

2. The next step is to create a structure at the top-management level to assist the top official in becoming involved and leading the company-wide effort. It ties in improvements, and the resources to achieve them, with expected benefits. It emphasizes ways to influence customers and achieve more effective management of people. It provides means for evaluating, controlling, and authorizing improvement initiatives. The structure includes a steering arm and internal diagnostic teams.

3. Next, the steering arm works on developing a new company philosophy and policy guidance proposal to be presented to the top official to enact the involvement philosophy. This proposal involves a new look at company values and at internal and external relationships. It is the ultimate responsibility of the top official to attain concensus with his staff peers, corporate superiors, and the Board of Directors.

4. The successful companies also learned that middle management has been a key to progress, or lack of it. To assure their support, it is important to involve middle managers, who may be suspicious of change, early in the sequence. Early involvement in acquiring background knowledge, soliciting comments on the new philosophy and guidance, and attendance at management workshops are in order.

5. The current American Industrial Revolution involves changing from management of work to management of people. However, most American managers lack the skills necessary to effectively involve and manage employees. The initiation of change must begin with attitudes. Attitudes, in turn, are dependent on the working environment and management style of a company. Management and supervisor workshops must be established to develop managers' skills for improving environments, management style, and attitudes once "existing" environments, management characteristics, and attitudes have been determined.

6. The steering arm arranges for a representative of department heads to form an internal diagnostic team to define attitudes, environments, incentives, and criteria for "desired" conditions, and to determine obstacles to employee involvement. This information is used in the Management Workshop for

developing skills to improve environments and attitudes and to motivate people. It is used for similar purposes in the Supervisor's Training Program. Management and supervisory skills are employed to change "existing" environments to "desired" environments.

7. The steering arm commissions an external diagnostic team to examine feedback from customers about measurements and judgments of company products, services, and systems. It examines findings on related topics from such sources as American and foreign trade associations, consumer journals, competitors, suppliers, independent test laboratories, stock analysts, and American and foreign registers. Recommended goals and plans are prepared to respond to the findings and feedback.

8. Concurrently, the steering arm also commissions the internal diagnostic team to do three functions. The first step is to gather employee perceptions about company products, services, and systems: problems, opportunities, and favorable features. This information is converted into recommended goals and plans. The second step is to develop findings from internal plant measurements and records involving quality and productivity (i.e.: internal quality audits, scrap and rework records, waiver requests, customer complaint records, and cost overruns). The findings are reviewed, particularly for repeat problems and core causes. These findings are also converted into recommended goals and plans. The third step is to develop opportunities for improving competence by reviewing the gathered information and findings. This information is utilized in the Management Workshop and the Supervisor's Training Program. Throughout this three-step process, the internal diagnostic team acts as the coordinator and uses management quality circles, supervisor/hourly employee quality circles and value engineering teams to acquire and update information and develop goals and plans.

9. The recommended goals and plans from both diagnostic teams are reviewed and evaluated, priorities are established, and available funds are allocated by the steering arm with approval of the top official. The internal diagnostic team then coordinates the same circles and value teams to implement approved and funded goals and plans. Achieving and maintaining a desired competitive position requires constant vigilance of competitors and customers. The process of improving products, services, and systems is a continuous one.

10. A quality systems diagnostic team is formed to change one-department quality control to company-wide quality control and to improve supplier and inspection systems.

11. During the sequence, there are efforts to revitalize the company's education and training programs for the quality control discipline and productivity practices.

Creating A Structure At The Top-Management Level

Below is a list and brief description of recommended positions and teams that are essential to support top-management's company-wide involvement and leadership.

- Steering arm
- Incentives and resources team
- Education and training leader
- "President's plan"
- Customer Ombudsman
- Internal diagnostic teams
- Customer and external diagnostic teams

The Steering Arm

The top official usually appoints three individuals, who normally report to him, to act as the steering arm. The logical initial assignments to the steering arm are the members of the top official's staff responsible for quality control, human resources, and another major function, such as engineering or manufacturing. After a minimum assignment of a year, there can be replacements by other members of the top official's staff. The assignment is usually in addition to normal duties. Some companies make permanent assignments. The steering arm's initial activity is to assist the top official in acquiring background knowledge. This is usually done by reporting on visits to other companies or meeting with consultants.

The steering arm also provides and develops options for a new company philosophy. External research and many internal meetings are conducted to evolve company values and define desired relationships with employees, customers, and suppliers, as well as the Federal Government and community and local governments. While the steering arm develops options and makes recommendations, it is the top official who must decide and achieve final consensus with superiors and his staff.

It is important that the top official and his steering arm provide for early involvement of middle managers. The top official should communicate with middle management about acquiring background knowledge, making recommendations on the proposed new philosophy, and providing input on policy guidance. However, it is the steering arm that takes action.

Based on the new philosophy and policy guidance, the steering arm provides support to the internal diagnostic team while it is acquiring knowledge about "existing" company environments, attitudes, and obstacles to employee involvement. The steering arm evaluates the goals and plans recommended by the team, placing emphasis on long-term major benefits, applies the Pareto principle in order to give priority to the more vital benefits, allocates funding, as available, from the incentives and resources team, and implements an approval process with the top official. It coordinates the availability of funds and other resources with the incentives and resources team. The steering arm also provides findings, recommendations, and approval to the leaders of the Management Workshop and the Supervisor's Training Program.

Once compiled, the steering arm reports on the recommendations and initiates the approval process with the top official. Approved goals, plans, and funds are incorporated in the "president's plan" of which the steering arm is custodian. There are no annual lump authorizations.

The process of improving quality and productivity is a continuing one, forced by competitors' actions or ongoing desires of customers. There are also long- and short-range authorizations, high- and not-so-high priorities, and steering arm status and progress reviews sometimes resulting in redirection.

Change from "one-department" to "company-wide" quality control is needed. There have long existed some nonproductive relationships and practices externally between a company and suppliers and within a company between quality control engineers and purchasing agents. There have also been nonproductive practices in the total inspection system from initiation of manufacturing planning by suppliers or by a company, through final assembly, test, and delivery. This includes insufficient use of statistical controls. The steering arm recommends appointments to a quality systems breakthrough team and provides direction and control of these activities.

The Incentives and Resources Team

The incentives and resources team is also composed of individuals who report to the top official. Initial appointments to the team usually include the finance officer, the marketing manager, and a head of a major functional department. The incentives and resource team assists the top official in two ways. The first is to investigate existing company incentive, profit sharing, and recognition programs, and the programs of other companies. The second is to coordinate finance, marketing, and other department heads to develop funding for the investments to improve environments, provide incentives, and improve products, services and systems. The result of the team's efforts to develop funding is the identification of items reserved for the investments in the company's budget. There is continuous close coordination with the steering arm.

The team reports to the top official findings about the adequacy of existing programs and good and bad features of other programs investigated. It reports recommendations and coordinates implementation of the decisions made by the top official.

Education and Training Leader

The top official usually retains a quality control expert who reports directly to him, despite the change from "one-department" to "company-wide" quality control. A major responsibility of this expert is to lead and coordinate the company-wide quality control education and training program, the Management Workshop, and the Supervisor's Training Program covered in earlier chapters. This includes a program for top officials, upper managers, professional employees, supervisors, and workers from all departments. As a likely member of the quality control breakthrough team, described later, he or she will be knowledgeable of the changes to the quality control system developed by this team. The education and training leader is also responsible for enhancing relationships with universities and professional societies to achieve the unity and strength comparable to the Japanese.

The "President's Plan"

The "president's plan" is a concept of Japanese management particularly adaptable to this effort because it clearly shows the involvement and leadership of the top official and the participation of his staff. The steering arm reports findings and recommendations to the top official that originate with the internal and external diagnostic teams. It is the activities approved by the top official that are entered in the "president's plan." The plan is the authority to initiate work and release funds. It also controls the work and funds. Periodic reviews of activities result in a continued status, re-direction, or cancellation of plan actions.

The plan should include:

- Short- and long-range goals
- Brief description of actions
- Expected benefits
- Identification of funds and other resources
- Assignees
- Status (i.e., continuing, completed, re-directed, or cancelled).

The plan is not intended as a means to monitor detailed schedules. Infrequent but in-depth reviews are conducted by the steering arm to ascertain status and progress.

The plan is intended as a means of opening communication lines throughout the company. To this end, the plan should also include the new company philosophy and policy guidance and a summary of company incentive, profit sharing, and recognition programs.

APPOINTING THE DEPARTMENT HEADS' DIAGNOSTIC TEAMS

The direction and authority of the top official and guidance by the steering arm is implemented by diagnostic teams. Conflict with line management is avoided when the teams are composed of individuals reporting to and recommended by the department heads. Each department head proposes his representative. The top official appoints members and appoints chairpersons. Most organizations are handicapped by conventional organizations that separate functions, although most company activities need the combined help of several functions as a team. The diagnostic teams, like all other teams and circles, are composed of members from several functions. Yet, each team member is expected to coordinate with his superior, a department head.

The Internal Diagnostic Team

The internal diagnostic team has three functions. Early in the game, the team leads and coordinates the acquisition of knowledge about existing attitudes, environments, obstacles to employee involvement, and criteria for desired conditions. The team reports findings and recommends goals and plans to achieve desired conditions. When authorized, the team leads and coordinates implementation of approved goals and plans.

A second function of this team is to analyze the sources for achieving superior competence, and adapting concepts and techniques for application by company employees. The team is assisted by instructors from the Management Workshop and the Supervisor's Training Program.

The team's third function is to learn about acceptable features, problems, and opportunities for improvement within the company. Primary findings and recommended goals and plans come from management quality circles, supervisor/hourly employee quality circles, and value engineering teams. The team also reviews company measurements and records such as quality audits, scrap and rework records, waiver requests, cost overrun reports, and customer complaint correspondence.

The Customer and External Diagnostic Team

The customer and external diagnostic team is composed of representatives from marketing, finance, quality control and individuals from other departments who have customer contact.

The initial activity of the team is to research customer measurements and feedback contained in the plant's files. From this research, plans can be made for interviews with key customer personnel such as the contracts officer or quality control auditors. The purpose is to evaluate customer needs for improving quality and productivity. Findings and recommended goals and plans are submitted to the steering arm for evaluation and ultimately the approval process.

Another function of the team is to research reports and articles from external sources and conduct interviews where appropriate. Again, findings and recommended goals and plans are reported to the steering arm. The approved goals and plans are implemented by the internal diagnostic team.

The Quality Systems Breakthrough Team

There are many relationships between a company and its suppliers that are nonproductive for both parties. Japanese companies have superior relations with their suppliers. Some concepts are feasible and can be adapted for American usage. Some long-term nonproductive activities and procedures simply suffer from lack of attention and objective communication. Relations between quality control engineers and purchasing agents are often more like adversaries than a team. There has been long-term need to improve the quality system for suppliers that will result in substantial increases in quality and reductions to cost for both a company and its suppliers. This is one of two major reasons for establishing the quality systems breakthrough team.

The second major reason is a need for review of and improvements to the inspection system from the early planning phases through final assembly, test, and delivery. Wise, increased use of statistical controls can reduce the need for inspection, as can more self-monitoring by operators. More application of the "fitness-for-use concept" can reduce scrap and rework. The above improvements to the supplier quality control system can reduce costs and the need for re-inspection and re-test, as well as increase quality.

The greatest challenge to the team is to change from "one-department" to "company-wide" quality control. They will conduct studies, review existing directives and procedures, determine the best application of statistical controls, and investigate revised roles. They will develop new written instructions and evolve implementation of improved systems.

The top official, with advice from the steering arm, should appoint the quality systems breakthrough team. The chairman must be capable of creating unity among members who have different priorities and viewpoints. It is important that he or she have a broad understanding of quality control and an open mind. An obvious candidate may be a senior manager in engineering. Members should consist of senior managers in quality control, purchasing, manufacturing and engineering, and one or more well-qualified statisticians.

The Customer Ombudsman

The total effort described in this book is to influence customers and gain larger market shares. To this end, the establishment of an "Ombudsman" for the customer can result in major dividends for both the customer and the supplier company.

The top official arranges the Ombudsman appointment with his opposite number in the customer's organization. It is essential that the customer trust and have respect for the appointee. To assure effective and timely communication, an open-door policy is necessary and approved by the customer's top official and the top official of the supplier.

The primary function of the Ombudsman is to learn of emerging major problems and prevent their growth by alerting customer's and the supplier's top officials. The second major function is to learn information about competitors and track changing needs of the customer. The third major function is to learn who, in the customer complex, is particularly satisfied or dissatisfied with the supplier's products, services, or systems and why.

When the customer is in a foreign country, an expanded version of an Ombudsman should be considered. This is because marketing requires unique talents in most foreign countries, and these talents are hard to obtain. The concept is to create a small group of people who are particularly knowledgeable of a country's culture, language, its people, and the country's normal marketing practices, and assign marketing and sales functions to them. Implementation of contracts is done by a separate organization.

CHAPTER 8
IDENTIFYING EXISTING ATTITUDES, OBSTACLES, MANAGEMENT STYLES, AND ENVIRONMENTAL CONDITIONS

Introduction

The first step for improving environmental conditions is to identify the existing conditions and those conditions that need improvement. Identifying existing conditions can be achieved by using one or more of the methods below, which will be described in more detail throughout the remainder of this chapter. They include:

- Attitude surveys.

- Review of appraisal and exit interviews.

- Identification of obstacles.

- Survey of characteristics of management and supervision.

- Study of incentives and rewards.

- Study of company facilities available for work experimentation and for recreation/exercise.

After the existing conditions have been identified, they should be compared to desirable conditions previously covered in this book. From the results of the comparison, goals can be set and action plans outlined to change undesirable existing conditions. The final step is implementation of these goals and plans.

Both the Management Workshop and the Supervisor's Training Program (see Chapters 4-6) established skills, techniques, and criteria that will help implement the above steps. Chapter 7 also describes how the steering arm provides guidance to the internal diagnostic team, which determines findings of existing conditions and recommends goals and plans. The steering arm, via the president's plan, further provides the controls, by means of an approval process, and the release of authority and resources necessary to make the recommended revisions.

Note: The approach described by this book has been applied successfully by many companies. Some use names different than steering arm, diagnostic team and president's plan, but have similar structure and functions. There is no intent to promote use of the names.

ATTITUDE SURVEYS

Attitude surveys not only describe the positive and negative attitudes of the people, but also the causes of those attitudes. These include obstacles and opportunities for involvement, good and bad supervisor's and manager's characteristics, positive and negative findings about other environmental elements, and the fairness or lack of fairness of compensation, incentives and rewards.

We are concerned with achieving more effective involvement for all company employees. The attitude survey should be given to samples of all employees, including hourly, supervisory, professional, technical, and management people.

Many large corporations have their own professional groups who specialize in the conduct, analysis and reporting of attitude surveys. However, most surveys are done by independent contractors skilled in these techniques. It would be logical for the steering arm to delegate the arrangements for and administration of attitude surveys to the head of the personnel department.

Initially, reports should be released only to the steering arm, the top official, and immediate members of his staff. It is important to advise employees of results and the company's intent to provide and implement plans in response to the survey within a reasonable period of time. It is important to review the results along with other homework to develop short- and long-range actions. Quickie solutions neatly listed by each finding destroy credibility and contribute little to improve employee attitudes. Carefully prepared long-range solutions are essential to changing attitudes. When development of responses is delegated to lower echelons of management, the quickie solutions are more likely to occur. There must be participation by top line managers if credible and long-term results are to be achieved.

APPRAISAL INTERVIEWS

The appraisal interview provides an excellent opportunity for the development of mutual trust between managers, supervisors and employees. When the interview is done correctly, the manager or supervisor learns a wealth of information about the employee's attitude and elements of his environment, and the employee receives valuable feedback on his or her performance.

Dr. Norman F. Maier, author of *The Appraisal Interview-Objectives: Methods and Skills*, describes three techniques usually used for appraisal interviews. While the first technique is occasionally needed, the second and third provide the most information.

The Tell and Sell Technique
The interviewer assumes the role of judge. He communicates his evaluation to the employee and tries to persuade the employee to improve. He uses the attitude that people profit from criticism and appreciate help.

The Tell and Listen Technique
This is similar to the "Tell and Sell Technique" except that the interviewer listens to the interviewee's side of the story. Input from the interviewer may possibly change the interviewer's judgment.

The Problem Solving Technique
This technique places the interviewer in the position of helper. Problems involving job performance are discussed, and since experience and views are pooled, both sides gain from it. The increased freedom and responsibility will create positive motivation for the employee. The exercise on "Nondirective Interviews" from the Management Workshop provides guidance for the "Problem Solving Technique."

The last two categories are the source of a sizable volume of information about existing conditions. It is when technique three is used properly that a manager not only evaluates performance but also learns the obstacles and conditions that have affected the performance and the attitude of the employee.

Appraisals are sensitive, so only those authorized personnel department employees can conduct the reviews and analyses. Normally the steering arm delegates this task to the head of the personnel department. It is important that the reviewers are indoctrinated into the guidelines and criteria for conducting appraisals provided by the Management Workshop.

The reviewers should be assigned two objectives. The first is to review and analyze appraisals to develop findings about employee attitudes, the obstacles preventing effective performance, and the conditions that motivate or demotivate the employee. The findings should be based on review and analysis of cumulative data. Particular attention should be given to identifying root causes of obstacles, repeatability of findings, and distinguishing between the few vital obstacles and the many trivial obstacles. Findings should be localized to areas or organizations when possible. Recommendations should accompany findings.

The second objective is to review existing procedures for preparation of position guides, performance factors and appraisals. Compliance to these procedures is to be evaluated and findings developed. Compare findings with the guidance and criteria for appraisals provided by the Management Workshop, and make recommendations for improving procedures and instructions. Distribution of the reports should be restricted to the top official, his staff and his steering arm. The steering arm will evaluate the findings and recommendations about obstacles, conditions and attitudes with reports from the attitude survey and other homework. The steering arm will also evaluate the findings and recommendations on compliance with existing procedures and those on appraisal procedures. The intent is to review and analyze appraisals as a continuing means to determine obstacles, conditions and attitudes. The more the appraisal system is improved, the better the source of information. Action to improve the system will be directed by the steering arm. For those recommendations that are approved, resources will be authorized for short- and long-range action.

EXIT INTERVIEWS

Exit interviews can reveal more vital information about obstacles and existing conditions. There is only one objective for exit interviews — to define the reason for termination. It is essential that the interview be conducted by an unbiased third party. The review should be assigned and reported the same way as appraisal reviews, and findings and recommendations are used in the same way as those from the appraisal review.

OBSTACLES

There are obstacles to achieving quality of products or services which are caused by top officials and are seldom addressed. There are other typical obstacles caused by middle and front line managers that are better understood but still require attention. The obstacles caused by top officials can result in unintentional loss of business and often cannot be remedied before the damage is done. Such obstacles often occur when the board of directors or other authority appoints a top official based on the current needs of the company. The need may be for an individual with a background in finance, technology, marketing or law. Naturally, that person may lack experience, knowledge and interest in quality control.

What causes these obstacles? First we must recognize that the actions and interests of the top official affect the quality of the company's products and services more than any other factor. Each of the examples described below has occurred in company after company. They have been a primary reason for the decline of our national and international reputation for quality.

The following may cause obstacles to quality products or services:

- Increased attention and resources applied to other high priority needs of the company resulting in too drastic cuts in attention and resources to assure quality.

- Awards by the top official in terms of promotions, perks, recognition and money for many kinds of accomplishments, but no awards for improvements to quality.

- Reduction in funding and support for company-sponsored education and training programs for quality control. Company-sponsored programs remain the principal source of training for quality control.

- The philosophy of the board of directors or superior corporate officials is to attain short-range profits and returns on investments as quickly as possible with expectations of increases every quarter.

- Conflicts between schedule and quality are continuously argued among all echelons of management and never resolved at the top.

- Mergers, shakeups and/or need for fast expansion result in major and frequent changes in management without consideration for maintaining quality.

- Assumptions that good design precludes the need for further attention to quality. Poor quality, however, is usually introduced in procurement from suppliers, and in manufacture, assembly and testing.

Obstacles are created when the causes result in loss of top quality control managers, along with the best quality control engineers. Word spreads fast, not only in the quality control community, but also through other channels to customers, suppliers and competitors. Suppliers begin to follow the example of the company. Their incoming material has to be reworked more often, causing higher customer costs. Competitors' proposals emphasize their quality. Within the company, needed capital equipment for manufacturing, testing and inspecting products cannot be obtained. Standards and calibration retrenchment cause surprising obstacles. The ultimate impact is loss of quality reputation with customers and then loss of business.

When it comes to solutions, we are faced with two conditions. One is the long-term effort to regain our eminent national and international competitive position for quality. The other is to cope better when it is necessary to install a top official with little background or interest in quality.

Solutions must come from top management. Some suggestions are:

- Install top officials with manufacturing backgrounds if appropriate. If not, strengthen quality leadership within top management.

- Improve the company-sponsored education and training program for quality control.

- Develop or recruit highly qualified key quality control specialists.

- Utilize supportive institutions. Universities and the American Society for Quality Control have increased their capabilities to help educate, train and provide other means to support industry. Tell them your needs for support and use them.

- Have the top official make the company's commitment to quality known to the customers, to the suppliers, and throughout the company.

- Establish the position of Customer Ombudsman, described in Chapter 7, using an individual with quality control background.

- Reward accomplishments for quality comparable with rewards for other reasons.

- Do not establish a motivation program with hoopla, posters and prolific certificates of appreciation. Do create short-term objectives for keeping the quality train on the tracks during transition periods. Then create long-term objectives for improving quality and productivity of products, services and systems.

- Direct middle management to correct obstacles caused by middle and front line managers described below.

Most companies have many obstacles, correctable by middle managers, which prevent employees from applying their full potential to improving quality and productivity. They are often due to organization, poor management practices and the existing environment. We already have a list of obstacles from the exercises from the Management Workshop and the Supervisor's Training Program and findings about existing environmental conditions. Analysis of attitude surveys and appraisal and exit interviews add to the list. There is another important source for identifying obstacles and learning other existing environmental elements which affect employees' performance. Most obstacles and environmental conditions involve several organizations and functions. Discussion among all representatives results in more accurate and less emotional findings and recommendations.

The other important source is an Americanized version of quality circles, which can be applied to all categories of employees and managers. Each circle can be composed of representatives from several organizations and functions. An objective authority, such as the internal diagnostic team, can recommend where circles are most needed, how many circles to form, and the leadership and membership. The circles should be advised to look for repeating patterns, and to seek root causes of obstacles and conditions. They can apply the Pareto principle and search for the few vital obstacles and conditions, disregarding the trivial. Findings and recommendations from the circles should be evaluated and commented on by the internal diagnostic team before forwarding to the steering arm.

Examples of obstacles found in a typical company that can be corrected by middle managers are:

- Lack of understanding about job responsibilities.
- Lack of knowledge about what constitutes acceptable work.
- Procedures prepared to impress auditors which are of little use to operators and inspectors.
- Written instructions that are either difficult to understand, impractical to apply, or are not relevant.
- Satisfactory specifications which are misapplied.
- Rigid enforcement of specifications when a "fitness-for-use" concept should apply.
- Multiplicity of conflicting instructions from manuals published by several different organizations.
- Poorly maintained and calibrated tools and instruments.
- Unavailability of test and inspection data from suppliers.
- Lengthy waiver approval process.
- Lack of policies and decisions to resolve conflicts between schedule and quality.
- Lack of knowledge of who to turn to for instruction in resolving problems.

- Insufficient instruction or standards covering cosmetic defects.
- Insufficient lead times for orders of "state-of-the-art" or complex components.
- Insufficient time allotted for first article inspection.

CHARACTERISTICS OF MANAGEMENT AND SUPERVISION

The Likert Management Characteristics (Figure 5.3) describes criteria for desired characteristics of management and supervision. It also enables measurement of existing characteristics. From the Management Workshop, we have a significant range of measurements of each front line manager by several of his supervisors. We have the same information for each manager from several of the subordinate managers. We lack similar information from professional employees about their managers and from hourly employees about their supervisors.

There are two techniques for acquiring such information from professional employees. The first uses the "skip level" technique: the manager's manager meets with a sample of professional employees to obtain their evaluations of their manager using the Likert matrix. When intended use of this technique is discussed, there is usually a strong reaction about undercutting immediate managers. After application, there is usually recognition that it is an objective way to acquire the information. Further, it is recognized that the results benefit employees, the manager and his manager, when used in a positive way. The second technique substitutes individuals from the personnel department for the manager's manager.

Usable information is obtained from hourly employees in a simpler and more direct manner. At a regular round table meeting the supervisor asks his employees to complete the motivation questionnaire from the Management Workshop. It is less complex than the Likert matrix and also less personal.

The information is primarily used by individual managers and supervisors. Each should establish his or her goals for achieving desired characteristics.

However, top management can help improve characteristics through education and training programs, policies about position guides, appraisal interviews and other means. The personnel department should be charged with analyzing all measurements and preparing profiles of existing characteristics applicable to organizations, each echelon of management and the total company. These analyses and profiles can be used both for improving characteristics and as a base to compare future improvement or lack thereof. This information should be made available to the top official, his immediate staff and his steering arm.

STUDY OF INCENTIVES AND REWARDS

The emerging industrial revolution that makes more effective use of employees must include the consideration that extra effort deserves extra rewards. Both managers and employees recognize that added profits should be shared with the employees who made the added effort. More and more companies have developed various means for sharing profits. They range from establishing set percentages of profits to be awarded to select employees to detailed work incentives applicable to each employee.

Many companies need to review their programs for incentives and rewards related to expectations for the added effort. The top official's incentives and resources team is an appropriate agency to conduct this study. Normally, it will not take the team long to learn about company programs. They will probably range from cost improvement and suggestion award programs, through incentive and recognition programs, to and including executive compensations.

When all the existing incentive and reward programs are identified, they can be evaluated for purpose and effectiveness. An improved incentive and reward program can then be developed. Guidance comes from the studies of employee needs by Maslow, Herzberg, and McGregor. Over the years there has been little challenge to these studies except for money as motivation. They categorize needs into those that achieve high motivation, those that provide floor or maintenance needs (which are expected but don't particularly motivate) and those that demotivate. Money is included in the floor or maintenance needs. Many managers and heads of personnel departments disagree. We agree with the concept that if executives are awarded added financial compensation for their added contribution, then other employees should be awarded additional money for theirs. It has been demonstrated that executives are substantially motivated by money.

Guidance also comes from a Theory Y assumption of McGregor, i.e., "Commitment to objectives is a function of the award associated with their achievement." More recently it has been stated that the greatest management principal in the world" is "what gets rewarded gets done." Other guides are the new company philosophy and the balanced objectives that consider both company and employee interests. Chapter 16, Communication and Rewards, also provides ideas. It is beyond the scope of this book to present all of the recently developed options for profit sharing. In most cases there has not been sufficient time to appraise their relative value. The incentives and rewards team should rely heavily on company philosophy, objectives and conditions and tailor an improved incentives and reward program to them.

STUDY OF COMPANY FACILITIES FOR EXPERIMENTATION AND RECREATION

Some companies provide small, separate workshops or laboratories that employees may use to pursue some improvements to quality or producibility. Other companies provide recreational and/or exercise facilities for use by employees. Most provide employee libraries.

This study identifies such facilities, indicates what category of employee uses the facility, and provides comments on extent of use. The steering arm can assign this study to a management quality circle. The circle should report findings and make recommendations to the steering arm about additions to or further use of these types of facilities.

CHAPTER 9
CHANGING ATTITUDES, REMOVING OBSTACLES, AND IMPROVING THE ENVIRONMENT

Introduction

From the preceding chapter and the workshops we have learned how to identify existing attitudes, obstacles, environments and management styles. We know criteria for desired conditions from the workshops. This chapter provides guidance to managers for changing and improving the existing environment.

CHANGING ATTITUDES
Program Vs. An Additional Management Discipline

The era of extravagant motivation programs is over. It has been replaced by the approach that more effective use of employees is achieved by new management concepts and associated discipline. The concepts and discipline are simply continuous normal tools of management. Companies who have demonstrated superiority or equality with Japanese competitors have applied this approach.

The demise of the major programs approach was because they were only effective over short periods of time. Excess hoopla resulted in demotivation, and exaggerated measurements of accomplishments caused lack of credibility. However, the programs achieved substantial increases in quality and productivity, though effective only for short periods.

There is a place for the program approach within the framework of the new discipline. Some person, event or condition may introduce a high priority, short-term issue deserving special attention. Investigation can result in such findings with the recommendation that a short-term "program" be established. It would be processed as other findings and recommendations are processed. However, explanation of why the issue needs special attention and the short duration should substitute for flamboyant hoopla. Arrangements need to be made to verify measurements of accomplishments to preclude loss of credibility.

Human Nature

The intent is not to change human nature but to take advantage of human nature. We understand the Bible and ancient history because there has been little change in human nature since then. It is not likely that we can do things to change human

135

nature next year or the year after. Maslow, Herzberg, McGregor, *your* best manager, and the Japanese manager know most employees want to work and achieve high quality and productivity, and simply let them. Where the occasional manager or employee has the extreme negative characteristics of Theory X as a part of their human nature, they are unlikely to change. They must be given a different kind of job assignment or be terminated.

We note the large quantity of company findings and recommendations for removing obstacles, changing attitudes, and improving existing environments and may be concerned with how to cope with them. We will learn later these are spread out over time. We will also note that a great number of employees are involved with the many findings and recommendations. They are the ones who do most of the time-consuming work of investigation, goal setting, planning and implementation. Experience has shown that if they are given trust and allowed self-control, they will cope satisfactorily with only few controls. It is their human nature.

Sensitivity Training

The Management Workshop describes some new concepts, theories and principles for management and teaches skills and techniques for application. It does not emphasize sensitivity training.

Sensitivity training peaked in the '60s. The National Training Laboratories became affiliated with the National Education Association and they offered sensitivity training. The Menninger Foundation, headed by Dr. Harry Levison, developed seminars for sensitivity training. Soon there were a hundred agencies providing sensitivity training. Tens of thousands of managers attended these in the '60s, and some still do today. However, the good effects have been offset by the bad effects. In many companies, sensitivity training was not the means to an end but the end itself. In others, the time and effort used for the training left no momentum to proceed to more practical applications to improve quality and productivity. Hence, sensitivity training is not emphasized. Removing obstacles and improving the environment are emphasized.

REMOVING OBSTACLES AND IMPROVING THE ENVIRONMENT
Time

It is possible to get the impression that all of the investigations are completed at the same time and all the findings and recommendations are forwarded to the steering arm at the same time. Let us examine what we are trying to do and we will see this is not true.

Our primary concerns are the vital obstacles and environmental changes that impact employee involvement. By their nature, long-range plans and actions are needed to resolve them. Usually, each requires different individuals and different time periods for investigation, goal setting, planning and implementation. Other obstacles and environmental changes involve shorter time periods of various durations. Some investigations are given high priority and others, with lower priority, may be delayed awaiting resources. Of particular importance, constant vigilance is needed to detect introductions of new obstacles or negative environmental conditions. It is a never-ending process. In addition, while the steps to initiate investigations and obtain approvals and resources are few and simple, often they must be iterated. The process is spread over time and is of a continuous nature, year after year.

Steps To Remove Obstacles And Improve Existing Conditions

Now the steps to remove obstacles and improve existing conditions can be better understood. The steps are few and simple. They apply to all your company's findings and recommendations.

Step 1. Initiating Investigations

Most investigations are performed by managers, particularly the internal diagnostic team whose members are managers representing department heads, and the managers' quality circles to whom they delegate. However, before managers can act, they often need information about the obstacles and environmental conditions that impact supervisors and hourly employees. To obtain this information, the internal diagnostic team organizes supervisor/hourly employee quality circles.

Step 2. Findings And Recommendations

All sources should be instructed about root causes, repeatability, and the need to discriminate between the vital few and the trivial many. All reports should summarize findings and recommendations. They should be forwarded to the internal diagnostic team, except for sensitive reports by the personnel department, which go directly to the steering arm.

Step 3. Evaluations And The Approval Process

The internal diagnostic team should comment and add their recommendations for each report.

The steering arm will evaluate all findings and recommendations and execute its approval/disapproval. The top official provides guidance about issues for which approval authority is not delegated to the steering arm.

For approved items that require resources, the steering arm consults with the incentives and resources team, which affects decisions and priorities. Once again, the steering arm obtains the top official's approval or disapproval.

All approved recommendations, altered recommendations, and resources, where dictated, are entered in the president's plan, which is authority for action.

Step 4. Goals And Plans

Generally, approved recommendations are returned to the parties who made them or to whom they apply. Those parties prepare goals and plans. Where specified, they are required to obtain a second approval of goals and plans as directed. Otherwise they proceed to implementation.

Step 5. Progress And Status

Detailed monitoring is not intended. Ample freedom and self-control are allowed. Assignees report completions or failure to continue, which are recorded in the president's plan.

The steering arm, at infrequent periods, such as quarterly or semi-annually, should review progress and status. There should be entries in the president's plan indicating the status of recommendations: continuing, completed, redirected or cancelled.

CHAPTER 10
CUSTOMER AND OTHER EXTERNAL JUDGMENTS OF QUALITY AND PRODUCTIVITY
FROM IMPROVING THE ENVIRONMENT TO IMPROVING QUALITY AND PRODUCTIVITY

The sequence described in Chapter 9 prescribes that attitudes must first be changed, obstacles removed, and the environment improved. By itself, this results in increased self-motivation of employees and improvements in quality and productivity. After a good start has been made on this phase, we can then implement direct improvement of products, services and systems.

Up to now, we have implemented the Management Workshop and Supervisor's Training Program that have provided our leaders with skills and techniques. They have applied this learning and made a substantial start in removing obstacles, improving the environment and changing attitudes. It is neither necessary nor desirable to take the considerable time required to complete this phase before starting the next phase. When employees become convinced that the effort is genuine, they will respond readily to becoming more effectively involved improving products, services, systems of production and systems for providing services.

The structure for this next phase has been described in Chapter 7. It included the steering arm, the customer and external diagnostic team, the Customer Ombudsman and the internal diagnostic team.

About Objectives And Priorities

The chief executive officers of the best managed companies know (1) the most important objective of a company is to satisfy its customers; (2) continuous improvements in quality and producibility of products, services and systems are essential to satisfying the customer and increasing the company's share of their business; (3) the customer's needs and judgments about the company's ability to provide high quality products and services at less cost have far greater priority than internal judgments. These companies have found ways to learn customers' needs and judgments on a continuing basis.

Many companies still emphasize outmoded objectives. Initially all chief executive officers or their corporate superiors required periodic reports that presented only compilations of internal measurements of quality characteristics of products or services. Then, most followed a trend and required reports that emphasized "quality costs." Only a small percentage of American companies have recognized the importance of or developed effective ways to continuously learn customer needs and judgments for improving quality and productivity.

ACQUIRING CUSTOMER AND EXTERNAL NEEDS AND JUDGMENTS

This chapter describes ways used by some companies to effectively and continuously learn customer and external needs and judgments of a company's products or services. Initially the chief executive officer should explain the new objectives and processes to his customer's top official and request his cooperation. At the same time he can propose establishing the Customer Ombudsman. Care should be taken that the customer realizes the process is to improve quality and productivity and is not an audit to determine and correct deficiencies. Approval should be obtained for customer diagnostic team members to interview key customer officials.

The composition and charter of the customer and external diagnostic team was described in Chapter 7. The team should prepare for interviews of key customer officials by preliminary homework. This is the identification and study of existing customer documents in company files, and documents and journals from external sources. Examples of typical documents and journals from customers and external sources are given below:

Customer Documents

—Pre-Contract Award Surveys

—Complaint Letters

—Study Reports of Common Problems of the Industry

—Periodic or Special Surveys

—Records of Inspections or Tests on Delivered Products

—House Organ Articles on Competitors, Common Problems, and Equipment or Technology Breakthroughs

—Audits of Quality Control

—Finance Audits of Scrap and Rework Costs

—Performance Reports of Monitoring Agency

—Records of User Unsatisfactory Reports

—Minutes of Periodic Progress Meetings

—Assessment Reports of Standings Compared with Competitors

—Readiness Audits for New Regulations

Trade And Technical Society Documents

—Trade Journal Articles on Competitors, Common Problems, and Equipment or Technology Breakthroughs

—Reports from Technical Society Meetings on Competitor Presentations and Solutions to Problems

—Awards and Commendations to Competitors

Corporate Documents

—Strategic Business Plans

—Performance Surveys

—Minutes of State of the Business Meetings

—Annual Stockholders' Report

Other External Documents

—Consumer Reports

—Independent Test or Audit Agencies

—Stock Analyst's Reports

—Competitors' Advertisements

—Suppliers

—Polling Organizations

—Business Journals

—*Wall Street Journal*

Fortified with this preparatory homework, designated key team members should interview key customer officials. The name of the game is to listen.

When the user is someone different than the initial customer, the user's measurements, judgments and opinions must be obtained. Where possible this is done by interviews. Sometimes the interviewees are distributors. When there are numerous users, it is necessary to resort to polls. Polls can range from contracting with a firm that does polls, to self-designed polls using the Likert Scale learned in the Management Workshop, to simple letters requesting observations of needed improvements.

ANALYSIS AND REPORTING OF INFORMATION

On completion of interviews and acquisition of external information, drafts of findings and recommendations for improvements should be discussed with the full team. It is an excellent means of comparing information and obtaining added insights and perspectives, and it enables the team to improve final drafts of findings and recommendations.

Both written and oral reports that include specific findings and recommendations should be given to the steering arm, the top company official with the steering arm, and then to the top official's department heads. There should be substantial discussion and development of consensus of judgments with all the above parties before a report of findings is presented to the customer.

High priority should be given to responses to the findings. It is important to remind participants that efforts to continuously improve quality and productivity are vital in the competition with foreign as well as local companies. Tradeoffs must be studied between cost and expected returns. Additional research or studies may be required. Some improvements will deserve higher priority than others. Some improvements can be achieved in a short time period while others may require considerable time. Some are not worth doing and others can't be afforded at the time. It is vital that periodic oral and written progress reports be provided to the customer.

This represents a major initial step in a continuing process. The Customer Ombudsman will, from time to time, submit his observations and recommendations. Infrequently, he will initiate reassembly of the customer diagnostic team for general or targeted interviews. It is necessary that the same structure be maintained giving high priority to responding to customer's observations and reporting back to customers. While the process will become more routine, it must always be remembered that the objective is to satisfy the customer and obtain a larger share of his business.

CHAPTER 11
INTERNAL JUDGMENTS OF QUALITY AND PRODUCTIVITY
THE CHALLENGE

Most managers and other employees of a company have an impact on quality and all affect productivity. It is natural that the individual closest to the work should be aware of ways to improve the product, service, production systems or systems to provide services. Making more effective use of these individuals is America's greatest opportunity to improve quality, reduce costs and regain our international reputation. The challenge is to harness this huge quantity of knowledge from so many sources and make use of it.

The structure described in Chapter 7 handles this challenge. The task is easier because the obstacles hindering involvement by these individuals have been or are being removed.

The internal diagnostic team, formed by representatives of each department, supports the steering arm and coordinates the efforts of the quality circles, value engineering teams and individuals assigned to investigations. Each is usually formed by members from different functions and organizations, since most improvements require these varied contributions. The steering arm, with the approval of the top official and the concurrence of department heads, provides the direction that energizes the internal diagnostic team. Once employees realize that the company's genuine intent is to remove obstacles and improve the environment, this team can go to work. It is advisable, however, to wait until the steering arm has completed its evaluation and discussions of the initial report of the customer and external diagnostic team.

IDENTIFYING PROBLEMS AND OPPORTUNITIES TO IMPROVE QUALITY AND PRODUCTIVITY

All members of the internal diagnostic team should sharpen their knowledge and instincts about where major problems and opportunities are located and who are likely candidates to contribute solutions. They should have frequent consultations with their department heads, review the customer and external diagnostic team report and simply "wander around" to observe and ask questions.

A major source of potential problems and opportunities is documents in company files. Attention to these documents can increase quality and productivity:

—Internal Quality Audit Reports

—Scrap and Rework Records

143

—Quality Cost Reports

—Quality and Productivity Reports required by the Corporate Office or other superiors

—Annual Statements for Stockholders

—Customer Complaint Letters

—Waiver Request Records

—Incoming Inspection Reports covering material from suppliers

—Final Acceptance Records.

The chairman of the internal diagnostic team makes assignments for the study and analysis of these reports. He instructs assignees to: (1) Give particular care to determining root causes of problems and to noting repeat problems; (2) Document findings of problems and opportunities; (3) Identify individuals most likely to contribute to solving the problem or exploiting the opportunity for each finding; and (4) Apply the Pareto principle to distinguish which problems or opportunities are vital to the company's business and which have minor impact on the business.

The team then holds group discussions on drafts of the findings. This process permits introduction of new information, exchange of views and new insights. Eventually consensus about individual findings is reached and the final draft of the findings can be refined.

CLARIFYING QUALITY CIRCLES AND
VALUE ENGINEERING TEAMS

The next task of the internal diagnostic team is to select a few vital problems or opportunities and make assignments to a quality circle, value engineering team, or to one or two individuals. Their assignment is to analyze the problem or opportunity in depth, develop goals to solve the problem or exploit the opportunity, outline preliminary plans to meet the goals, and include estimate of costs and other required resources.

The terms quality circles and value engineering teams are used because each is associated with a discipline that assures an orderly and professional approach. However, we need to clarify when to use a quality circle and when a value engineering team should be used. Further, American business has had over a decade of experience applying quality circles with highly mixed results. It's necessary to take advantage of the lessons learned from that experience.

The following guidelines respond to lessons learned and can clarify the use of quality circles versus value engineering teams:

- Quality circles can include any individuals in the company who can make a contribution to the assignment. Normally there will be:
  - Manager Quality Circles
  - Supervisor/Hourly Employee Quality Circles
  Other circles can be formed as needed.

144

- An assignment will be made to a value engineering team if the problem or opportunity is technical in nature and requires the participation of professional employees. This usually involves a function requiring professional analysis to develop options for higher quality and/or lower cost.

- An assignment will be made to a quality circles team if the problem or opportunity involves production systems, systems for providing services, and policy, procedural or administrative matters not requiring significant involvement of professional personnel. Technical problems or opportunities will also be assigned to quality circles if within the capability of the supervisors, technicians or hourly employees. Such problems or opportunities may require a short period of consultation from professional personnel.

- Quality circles and value engineering teams are established by appointment by the internal diagnostic team or a department head. Any group that identifies a problem or opportunity should be encouraged to request designation as a circle or a team. It must be authorized by the internal diagnostic team or a department head.

- Quality circles and value engineering teams are disestablished on completion of their assignment unless there is an obvious follow-up assignment.

- An analytical and statistical control course is to be applied throughout the company and will replace similar training given circles or teams.

- Because there are not permanent circles or value engineering teams, it is impossible to provide in-depth training over extended time periods to individual teams. Instructors from the Management Workshop, or on retainer from nearby universities, can provide abbreviated indoctrination to all quality circles and value engineering teams.

Developing Goals And Preliminary Plans

Using the above guide, the internal diagnostic team assigns selected problems or opportunities to quality circles or value engineering teams. The team assures these groups have a suitable place to meet and work. The internal diagnostic team directs the circle or value engineering team to analyze the problem or opportunity in depth, develop goals to improve quality or productivity, and prepare preliminary plans including cost estimates. A member of the internal diagnostic team is assigned to offer guidance to the circle or value engineering team, and arranges for the indoctrination described under guides above.

Quality circles and value engineering teams are to be given the opportunity to present their results to the internal diagnostic team and other inside/outside experts qualified to judge. Suitable facilities for such informal presentations should be provided. If needed, additional work can be done as a result of comments and help received at the presentation. Goals and preliminary plans, including costs, should be documented. The report is submitted to the international diagnostic team, who reviews, comments and makes recommendations for each goal submitted and forwards the report to the steering arm.

Management Controls

The steering arm evaluates the submittal. The purposes of the evaluation are:

- To determine conformance with the philosophy and objectives of the company.

- To determine the probability of satisfying customer needs or concerns, maintaining current business or furthering future business.

- To achieve features and costs superior to competitors.

- To prevent a catastrophic effect on the business through a major failure in quality or an unplanned major increase in cost.

- To balance potential return and availability of funds and resources.

While it is essential to continuously improve the quality of a company's products and reduce its costs to be a successful competitor, there is the harsh reality of needing funds and resources to do it. The incentives and resources team that reports to the top official develops budgets for this work, makes the extra effort to identify usable funds within the company, and occasionally secures special grants from outside sources, such as federal grants or corporate funds. To approve a submittal, the steering arm must either authorize the funds and resources to do the work, or assure it can be done without additional funds or resources.

We need to take a new look at the axiom, "You can't get something for nothing." The new look is associated with a quotation from John W. Gardner, author of *Excellence: Work = Talent + Motivation*. In a company without a philosophy and with a poor environment and the usual obstacles, the cost of improvements is higher than when the reverse conditions exist. This has been demonstrated by our competitors and by the thousands of companies who implemented "motivation programs." The savings result from "making more effective use of employees" and the "motivation" part of the equation. You still don't get something for nothing. However, the cost for assuring a good environment and fewer obstacles is small compared to the extra work that results.

There is an approval and concurrence process within top management. Some degree of authority can be delegated to the steering arm and even the internal diagnostic team. The more vital and long-range submittals okayed by the steering arm must be approved by the top official. Such approval comes easier if the steering arm develops prior consensus with the involved department heads. Approved submittals are authorized by inclusion in the president's plan along with funds and resources where required. When approval and authorization occur, the internal diagnostic team coordinates the affected quality circles or value engineering teams in the plan's implementation.

Self-Control By Employees

Management does not monitor closely the accomplishment of the approved goals. The quality circles and value engineering teams determine their own milestones and schedules. They do have an obligation to inform the internal diagnostic team of changes in status, including completion, cancellation or major change in goals. They initiate oral or written progress reports. Progress and status of all approved submittals are reviewed annually or semi-annually by the diagnostic team and the status updated in the president's plan.

The Continuing Nature Of The Process

The initial investigations by the assignees may require a short period of time or many months. Implementation of approved goals also will require different lengths of time. Emphasis is placed on major, complex, vital issues and long-range solutions that correct core causes or provide substantial improvements. The effort is spread out over time.

It is a part of the internal diagnostic team's assignments to continuously identify problems and opportunities to improve quality and reduce costs. The process for handling each individual item as it occurs involves the same steps as described above. The need for improvements may lessen but it will always be there. Improvement is a continuing process.

CHAPTER 12
BREAKTHROUGH INTO SUPPLIER QUALITY SYSTEMS

Major opportunities exist to improve quality and reduce costs by making changes to the quality control and purchasing systems for suppliers. It is an area where the Japanese have achieved superiority. The reasons are:

- Japanese companies do not have to repeat the tests done by the supplier on receipt of materials.

- Compared to American companies, Japanese companies have considerably less rework of incoming supplies.

- Japanese companies have fewer returns to suppliers for rework or replacement.

- Japanese companies have less material provided to them by their suppliers that must be scrapped.

- Japanese suppliers apply "just-in-time inventories," or close versions of this system, and save companies costs for storage and inventory control.

- Japanese companies are more effective in troubleshooting and corrective action, because of their knowledge of suppliers' inspection, test, corrective action, and other quality control systems.

- An environment of teamwork exists due to company philosophy and long-term relations between company and suppliers in Japan.

These comparisons can be translated to dollars and cents in additional costs to American companies which must be passed on to the consumer. They can also be translated into quality characteristics of products and services which are readily judged by consumers.

This chapter will explain how to set up a supplier quality system. First, there exists a myth in the world of American suppliers. Some suppliers believe it is in their best interest to supply materials without any evidence of their quality. Suppliers are usually willing to supply certification that the terms of the contract, including specifications, have been met. However, they resist providing the inspection, test, corrective action and other quality history of the material supplied. If supplied, it is often delivered well after delivery of the material and is suspect for accuracy and completeness. Many suppliers believe this practice results in higher profits for themselves, though greater costs and poorer quality are passed to the company and then to the consumer. For short-term contracts that only occur once, the suppliers do make more profits. But in the long run, it leads to deterioration of their quality reputation and eventual reduction of their business.

This myth, however, still exists in America. A company must realize that an early step must be taken to change attitudes of both the company and the suppliers. The company needs to extend the concept of "making more effective use of people" to "making more effective use of suppliers." This begins with a new company philosophy pertaining to suppliers. Then obstacles must be removed and the environment improved to achieve greater teamwork. It must be recognized that additional costs for incentives for the delivery of high quality materials with complete quality histories will occur. This will be offset by the money saved in eliminating duplicate inspection, rework, scrap, delays and other costs involved with delivery of poor or unknown quality materials.

REMOVING SUPPLIER OBSTACLES
TO IMPROVE THE ENVIRONMENT

Ways to remove obstacles and improve the environment include:

- Develop a new company philosophy and policies for suppliers.
- Replace the obstacles caused by conflicts within the company between purchasing, quality control and production control with teamwork, a united front, and adherence to the new company philosophy and policies.
- Develop trust through open communication. The top official should occasionally arrange meetings with all suppliers. He can tell them about the new policies and what he hopes to receive in return from suppliers. This communication can occur at "Annual Vendor Days," to share both information and to present awards.
- Appropriate letters from the top company official to the top official of the supplier. Often suppliers do an act of special service — or disservice — to a company, and letters are an indicator of the company's concern for positive relations with suppliers.
- Key managers in the supplier's organization, in some cases, can be invited to attend the Management Workshop.

SUPPLIER BREAKTHROUGH TEAM

When suppliers recognize that the intent of a company to remove obstacles and improve the environment is genuine, they are more receptive to becoming involved in improvements to the company/supplier relationship. Also, suppliers are aware of the continuing and increasing rate at which they are being replaced by foreign competitors. Suppliers should welcome improvements to the relationships and to the system. It is time to address who will remove obstacles, improve the environment and implement the improvement. The top official must supply the leadership. The steering arm and the incentives and rewards team can apply their functions to this work. Then a diagnostic team is needed. An appropriate title is "breakthrough team into the quality and purchasing systems."

Members of the team should include a manager and a senior professional from purchasing, quality control, production control and engineering. Leadership of the team is critical. It should be a top manager with background in the above functions, but currently independent organizationally from any of them. A workable alternate is to appoint the head of the engineering department. Objectivity and innovation can be furthered if one or two unbiased experts from universities or consulting firms are included. All company members should complete the Management Workshop and be thoroughly indoctrinated with the new company philosophy and policy for suppliers.

The steering arm should support the top official for the development of philosophy, policy and plans to remove obstacles and improve the environment. The breakthrough team can also provide substantial help. The major assignment of the team, however, should be to set goals, plan and implement ways to improve the system. The team should consider the following ways to improve the system:

- Review the purchasing manual and procedures and the quality control manual and procedures for conflict and unnecessary obstacles.

- Establish realistic policies for priorities between quality, costs and scheduling.

- Better managed companies have criteria for the selection of suppliers and a means to rate the performance of suppliers. If a company lacks these, they should develop them. In either case additions should be made to the criteria and to the ratings as follows:

    —Will the supplier agree, by contract, to supply inspection, test, corrective action and other quality history at the time his supplies are delivered?

    —Will the supplier agree to schedule deliveries to minimize inventory storage and control?

    —Will the supplier provide useful warranties for his products?

    —How well has the supplier performed against the criteria set up by the company?

- In many companies, the value of material and services provided by all the suppliers exceeds the value of those manufactured by the company. While the company's top official has an impressive array of top managers to give attention to the work within the company, a disproportionately lower echelon purchasing manager leads the attention given to all suppliers. The quality control, production control and engineering managers who must work as teammates with the purchasing manager are usually of an even lower echelon of management. This structure should be carefully evaluated. In those companies where there is strong leadership for dealing with suppliers, there is significantly greater effectiveness in the use of suppliers.

- Review existing contracts with suppliers and all existing procedures in all organizations for problems, voids, and improvement. This includes:

—Unsatisfactory provision of data and quality history.

—Agreements that allow company personnel to witness inspections and tests.

—Creating the means to apply the "fitness-for-use" concept.

—Quality improvement warranties.

—Provision for incentives.

—A realistic waiver system.

- Review company quality control inspection planning and test planning procedures in light of the availability of inspection, test data and other quality history information from suppliers.

- Set goals for improving the system. Then develop new model contracts and revised procedures to implement the goals.

- Categorize existing major suppliers by expected cooperation or resistance to changes.

This is an evolutionary process. Select a few cooperative suppliers whose contracts are to be renewed and try the improved system with them. After debugging, announcements can be made at a meeting of all suppliers about the improved system.

> "New Basic" — Continuous process of innovations, quality, and productivity improvements to products, services, and systems.

CHAPTER 13
BREAKTHROUGH INTO THE INSPECTION SYSTEM

Another major opportunity to improve quality and reduce costs is with the inspection system. A primary reason Japanese companies produce higher quality products at lower cost is because their system of inspection is better. Examples include:

- As discussed in the preceding chapter, suppliers provide their inspection and test data with their products. This lessens the need for retest and reinspection by the purchasing company. Also this allows more accurate and faster troubleshooting should a problem arise.

- Statistical controls are applied to a greater degree. This provides greater assurance of quality and reduces the requirements for inspection, which lowers labor costs.

- Adversarial relations between manufacturing managers and operators on the one side, and quality control managers and inspectors on the other, are replaced by teamwork, which leads to greater efficiency, providing more quality at lower cost. This is due to a deep-seated philosophy of cooperation toward a common goal, in Japanese companies.

- The Japanese make effective use of their quality circles. Operators and inspectors work as a team to improve quality and reduce costs of production, assembly and inspection.

- Trust in and self-control by operators reduces the need for inspectors.

- Discipline of the employees on the production line is unusually high. The story of firing a cannon in the space between assembly lines and not scratching anyone is true.

Several changes can be made in American inspection systems to make them more competitive. The proper approach to effect major changes is consistent throughout this book. First is the need to change attitudes. Following this, obstacles to change must be removed and the environment improved. Once accomplished, there can be more effective involvement of the employees in improving the inspection system.

MANUFACTURING PHILOSOPHIES

In most companies, the design engineers dress in one room, all manufacturing personnel in another, and the quality control people in the third. Each group "suits up" in different uniforms and gets ready for the fray. Unfortunately, there is no dressing room for umpires because there are not any. It's true there are often project leaders or program managers, but neither their authority nor their effectiveness match the need. The day-to-day struggle of manufacturing and assembly often occurs in an environment of antagonism because there is no effective company philosophy regarding priorities between quality, scheduling and costs.

In Japanese companies there are underlying philosophies — some written and others not — but all thoroughly understood. They provide fundamental guidance on major matters and extend to provide basic guidance for priorities between quality, scheduling and costs. In Japan, a manager can make a mistake that has serious effects on the company. There are consequences for making mistakes, but they are conditioned by the attitude that mistakes are part of the learning process. There is no threat of job loss. However, if a manager intentionally violates the basic philosophy of the company, he is dismissed from the job and the company. This has a great social impact, as well as career and economic impact, on the individual and his family.

It is this kind of company philosophy that can provide stability and guidance in American companies. It should, in particular, cover priorities between quality, scheduling and costs, stressing the basic common goals of both manufacturing and quality control personnel.

In Chapter 3, the need to develop such philosophies early in the sequence was described. It further advised that there would be the need to reiterate this philosophy from time to time, as new knowledge was obtained. The time is ripe for reiteration as we learn the needs for major changes in the inspection system, as well as the supplier quality control system covered in the preceding chapter.

ATTITUDES AND STATISTICS

There is another major change required in attitudes that is unique to the inspection system. It has to do with the application of statistics. The founders of the modern discipline of quality control emphasized the need to apply statistical controls. Several of the world's greatest statisticians were available and promoted the application of statistics to quality control. They included Dr. Walter A. Shewhart, founder of statistical control of quality, and Dr. W. Edwards Deming, the internationally renowned consultant who helped the Japanese achieve their industrial revolution.

However, only occasionally do we find American companies whose top management has exploited statistical controls to their full potential. Part of the reason is lack of knowledge. Many texts and articles treat statistics in a classical fashion which is of great appeal to the mathematician, but has little appeal to the manager. Another reason for this is ineffective communication and negative attitudes. Initially there is often unsatisfactory understanding between a top manager and a statistician. The top manager does not understand how statistics can be applied within the company, due to the manager's lack of knowledge. The statistician is ineffective in describing applications because he must first learn more about the operation of the company and the world in which the manager lives. Another reason has to do with prior experience with misapplication of statistics by unqualified statisticians or untrained professional employees. These obstacles must be addressed before the application of statistical controls can begin.

The best way for top management to address these problems is to visit companies who have successfully overcome the obstacles and applied statistical controls effectively. The Major Appliance Products Division of the General Electric Corporation has resolved these obstacles by "top-to-bottom" education and training in statistical controls. The program applies to all echelons of managers and to nearly all employees.

We can also make use of a concept practiced in Japan, and a book by Dr. Kaoru Ishikawa titled, *Guide to Quality Control*. Managers of Japanese companies believe that their supervisors and hourly workers are qualified to learn and apply analytical and statistical methods. The attitude in American companies is that such training and application should be reserved for professional employees. Most hourly workers in Japan and America are high school graduates. While standards for Japanese high school graduates have been higher than those in America for a quarter of a century, most American graduates are qualified to learn and apply such tools.

Dr. Ishikawa made a major contribution which we can take advantage of. He wrote his book in order to increase the effectiveness of quality circles composed of supervisors and hourly workers. It is an excellent presentation of analytical and statistical techniques. He also recommends the approach for its use: (1) self study, (2) discussion with group members that often included guest quality control engineers, and (3) applications to problem solving. The book is published in English and its use is rapidly spreading across the United States. It is important to note that Dr. Ishikawa learned in Japan what is also true in America—that most texts on statistics are overly technical and inappropriate for teaching in industry. This applies to professional employees as well as supervisors and hourly employees. Dr. Ishikawa is involved in another method to educate and motivate supervisors. This is the publication of a monthly magazine formerly known as *QC for Foremen* and now renamed *FQC*.

The Management Workshop and the Supervisor's Training Program contribute substantially to removing obstacles and improving the environment for inspection. The relationships between managers at all levels and key statisticians can be enhanced if the key statisticians attend the Management Workshop.

BREAKTHROUGH INSPECTION SYSTEM TEAM

After a reasonable start in removing obstacles and improving the environment, we can turn to the more effective use of people in making improvements to the inspection system. First we need to address who will lead and coordinate this effort. The top official, steering arm, and incentives and/or resources team. They pursue their functions as they apply to the inspection system. The new ingredient is appropriately titled the "breakthrough inspection system team." Membership should include the manufacturing manager and a leading manufacturing engineer, the quality control manager and a leading quality control engineer, and the engineering manager and leading design engineer. Leadership of the team and appointment of statistical and special representation is critical. The chairman of the team, preferably, should be a top manager with a background in manufacturing and quality control, but not currently a part of either organization. The need is for innovative thinking.

There must also be strong representation by statisticians. It is essential that the statisticians have had considerable success in applying statistical controls in industry. It is also essential he be articulate in describing statistical controls in terminology readily understood by the managers. If such an individual is not an employee of the company, the consultant from a university or consulting firm should be given several weeks opportunity to study and observe company operations before joining the team. Objective and unbiased contributions can also come from recognized quality control and statistical experts outside the company, such as, another division of the company, corporate headquarters, a university or consulting firm. The charge given to the team is to develop and implement changes to the inspection system that will result in superior quality and less cost than foreign or American competitors.

The approach of the team should follow a sequence as below:

1. Careful review of existing directives and procedures dealing with the inspection system as they currently exist in all manuals and books of procedures in engineering, manufacturing, purchasing and quality control departments.

2. Preparation of detailed flow charts that depict the current flow of work as specified by these written instructions.

3. The establishment of quality circles that include managers in engineering, manufacturing and quality control in each circle. In some cases marketing and purchasing managers need to be included. Their function is to investigate systems and procedural problems, and identify opportunities for improvement.

4. The establishment of quality circles composed of supervisors and hourly employees from both manufacturing and quality control organizations. They should be given freedom to investigate and make recommendations about any means to improve the procedures and inspection system.

5. Investigate typical opportunities for improvement found in many American companies, such as:

    • Major increases in application of statistical controls, including top-to-bottom education and training in statistics.

    • Support of top management in developing a company philosophy to guide priorities for quality, cost and schedule.

- Improving the adaptation of Japanese-style quality circles to American companies.

- Substantially improving procedures for "first article inspection."

- Seeking more opportunities for substituting self-control by operators for inspectors once attitudes are improved.

- Applying the "fitness-for-use" concept: when specified performance is only an estimate, see if measured performance of finished unit is "fit for use." This can save costs for changed drawings, manufacturing plans, rework, retest and reinspection.

- Check and remove conflicts in manuals and procedures in all organizations that affect quality.

- Be sure operators and inspectors understand the procedures prepared by "procedure writers."

Based on the findings and recommendations of the team and quality circles, plus the continued study of new flow charts, the breakthrough inspection team should initiate improvements to the system by preparing revised or new instructions and procedures. When satisfied with the above, they should provide oral and written reports to the steering arm, the top official and his staff. On their evaluation, direction for implementation will be provided by the president's plan.

CHAPTER 14
MUTUAL SUPPORT BETWEEN UNIVERSITIES AND CORPORATIONS TO IMPROVE QUALITY AND PRODUCTIVITY

Introduction

Alfred P. Sloan once addressed the mutual responsibility and opportunity between corporation and campus by saying, "When the annals of our time are recorded, it will most likely be found that the two greatest contributions of our time have been the U.S. university and the U.S. corporation: both mighty forces, both uniquely American. If these two forces can go forward together in understanding and cooperation, there is no problem beyond their joint power for resolution. If however, they choose to go their separate ways, there is no solution of any problem affecting either, that is likely to be long lasting."

This chapter is about these two forces together proposing solutions to one problem—America's need to regain its international reputation for quality and productivity. Both universities and corporations have great stakes in the outcome.

More effective mutual support can be achieved by:

1. Improving the motivation and talents of university graduates entering the job market.

2. Reinstating the quality control education and training program that originally won our eminent international position for quality—and improving it.

3. Adapting concepts used in Japan for mutual support between universities and industry.

4. Universities fulfilling several obvious needs of industry to improve quality and productivity.

5. Industry fulfilling several obvious needs of universities that will enable more effective involvement in quality and productivity.

However, the task of improving this mutual support between universities and industry is both being helped and handicapped by the recent proliferation of reports about education as a whole. These reports are motivating improvements to the many standards of our educational system that will gradually benefit industry. The reports generally presented negative findings about all facets of our education system. *But the reports were incomplete because they did not describe the positive activities that provide effective support between universities and industry.* The reports compared educational qualifications of American graduates available for the job market with those of other nations and found us lacking. *But the reports did not include evidence that America is second only to Japan in having close and effective relations and support between university professors and industry managers. In this respect, America is recognized as superior to all other trade deficit nations.* The five positive ways outlined above to increase mutual support and improve quality and productivity must be implemented in an environment established by the reports. It is necessary to gain further understanding and perspective about the reports before describing the five ways for improvement.

PERSPECTIVE

Never in the history of American education has there been more spirited controversy and attention given to its improvement.

U.S. Secretary of Education T. H. Bell appointed a National Commission on Excellence and Education that prepared a report in April 1983, "A Nation at Risk." The first paragraph is a good indication of the Commission's conclusions about educational conditions:

> "Our Nation is at risk. Our once unchallenged preeminence in commerce, industry, science, and technological innovation is being overtaken by competitors throughout the world. This report is concerned with only one of the many causes and dimensions of the problem, but it is the one that undergirds American prosperity, security, and civility. We report to the American people that while we can take justifiable pride in what our schools and colleges have historically accomplished and contributed to the United States and the well-being of its people, the educational foundations of our society are presently being eroded by a rising tide of mediocrity that threatens our very future as a Nation and a people. What was unimaginable a generation ago has begun to occur—others are matching and surpassing our educational attainments."

Within two years, over 350 reports were prepared by academicians, government and foundation officials in response to the Commission's report. Because the subject of aid by corporations to universities was treated lightly in these reports, an older report was acquired. The report is the *Handbook of Aid to Higher Education by Corporations, Major Foundations and the Federal Government*, prepared by the Council for Financial Aid to Education and sponsored by the Carnegie Corporation, the Ford Foundation, the Rockefeller Foundation and the Alfred P. Sloan Foundation. This 1972 report lists the many ways corporations have provided assistance to universities in the past. This illuminating and useful checklist is presented at the end of this chapter.

While nationwide attention has been focused on the negative conditions of education, neither "A Nation at Risk" nor the other 350 reports describe the positive relations and support that currently exist between universities and corporations. For example, current demographics indicate there are a greater number of individuals between 35 and 45 than the age group attending high school, colleges and universities. The need for reeducation and training of the 35-45 age group has been considerable and is being met largely by continuing education departments. Individual consultants from universities make major contributions as do centers for specialized education. Many universities provide research and some have unique facilities. All the concepts, principles and theories for improving the environment presented in earlier chapters came from university professors.

In perspective, universities and corporations have much to build on in their quest to improve quality and productivity.

Five Ways To Improve Mutual Support

1. Improve The Motivation And Talents Of University Graduates Entering The Job Market.

The report, "A Nation at Risk", and the subsequent 350 related reports deal with this subject. The need exists. The reports tell us how to meet the need.

The greatest progress is improvement of standards for curricula and teachers. The least progress is with university undergraduate courses in quality control.

2. Reinstate And Improve Quality Control Education And Training Programs.

America won its eminent international reputation for quality control because it developed and applied a powerful new discipline. The same discipline links high qaulity with high productivity.

Dr. A.V. Feigenbaum, of the General Electric Company, developed total quality control (TQC) in the early '50s. Dr. J.M. Juran, a consultant, also developed his quality control discipline in the early '50s. Both assisted the government in creating MIL-Q-9858A, which was the military requirement for a new discipline approved in 1961 by Secretary of Defense Robert S. McNamara. The systems were continuously improved. New concepts such as "quality costs" and "fitness for use" were added. Adaptations of the discipline to service industries were developed. Today Feigenbaum and Juran are leaders in the current quality control crusade.

Statistical controls were a part of the early disciplines. Unfortunately, the full potential for statistical quality controls are seldom reached, and most companies today do not apply the rigorous disciplines that placed us first in the competition. A primary reason for not adhering is lack of educated and trained people.

When the new disciplines were initiated, most of the education and training was done at the business or plant site. Corporations developed curricula and provided instructors and institutes or centers for educating and training the quality control personnel in its divisions. The programs were comprehensive and in-depth. Consultants introduced education and training to all sizes of companies. Later the American Society for Quality Control (ASQC) evolved an Education and Training Institute. A major survey of universities and colleges in the '60s revealed negligible activity in teaching quality control. As the importance of quality control has been demonstrated by Japan, universities have taken a new interest in teaching quality control subjects.

It is strongly recommended that new education and training programs be established, or existing programs be upgraded, to teach the rigorous discipline needed to reacquire America's reputation. Considering the state of quality control in most American companies, the challenge is immense. The university professor, the industry manager, and the ASQC professional each have contributions to make.

Recommended courses for a revitalized and improved quality control education and training program are:

- *Company-wide quality control systems —*
  Describe the subsystems, flow of work, operating procedures, and responsibilities. The system provides the glue for all the work and people who impact quality. (See Figure 14.1.)

- *Company-wide quality control management —*
  On a company-wide basis, the course covers the management of the system. It concerns strategic business planning, quality control planning, the management of subsystems work, coordination among organizations, and quality costs.

- *Upper management leadership and involvement —*
  The program should cover the subjects described in Chapter 7.

- *Quality control engineering —*
  As all disciplines require specialists, so does quality control. They are the quality control engineers. They must be educated as experts in the system. They must be expert in technical planning and capable of providing technical leadership in any of the subsystems and directing and conducting troubleshooting and corrective action operations.

- *Supervisor and worker seminars —*
  A program of seminars, round tables and self-taught courses designed specifically for supervisors and workers.

- *Statistical techniques and their application —*
  This is several courses with different levels of difficulty tailored to different categories of attendees. Categories range from upper managers to hourly workers.

- *Management Workshop —*
  Presented in Chapters 3, 4, and 5.

- *Supervisor's Training Program —*
  Presented in Chapters 3 and 6.

Today, corporations have more choices for location of facilities and sources of instructors. Universities, colleges, consultants, and ASQC have talents and resources that can be tapped.

3. Adapt Concepts From Japan.

Japanese professors generally are more frequently and closely involved with the work of a company and the world in which managers of a company operate. The involvement of the professors enables them to contribute more effectively. Therefore, company managers hold them in even higher esteem. Examples of concepts that enable more effective involvement are:

- *Auditing*

   University professors are members of the quality control audit team headed by the company president. This enables them to become familiar with the work areas, the people, products and services. They contribute as an outside, unbiased auditor on an internal audit team.

- *Training*

   The Japanese are almost religious about their zeal for training. Much of this training has to do with pragmatic matters that would not be covered in conventional text books. They may involve short- or long-term training of hourly employees or managers. Japanese professors respond to such needs and prepare special texts or curriculum to meet these needs.

- *Gathering Intelligence*

   Japanese professors often travel to other countries to learn new concepts or gather intelligence on new products or facilities. It widens their knowledge and provides another avenue for involvement within a company.

- *Quality Planning*

   The "president's plan" in Japan is the equivalent of the president's quality control plan. He uses professors from universities to contribute to his "president's plan" and other quality planning.

- *Consultants*

   The Japanese frequently use professors as consultants. In America, the tendency is to use only professors with special expertise.

4. Utilize Universities To Fulfill Needs Of Industry.

Introduction

American companies now live among determined and strongly motivated foreign competitors. They risk not only that the Japanese make automobiles more efficiently, that South Korea has developed the world's most efficient steel mill, and Germany now makes the best machine tools. America's companies face a more fundamental risk. Knowledge, learning, information, skilled intelligence and ideas are the basic raw materials of international commerce. Today they are rapidly and vigorously spreading throughout the world. This is the more fundamental risk and the challenge to universities to support industry.

Quality Control Basic Education

The most effective way universities can meet this challenge is to educate or help industry to educate personnel in the basic quality control discipline. This has been covered previously.

Expanded Functions

Universities have the facilities, ability to conduct studies of quality control systems, and the skills of teaching. They can support industry more effectively if their professors and instructors become more involved in the work of industry and the world in which managers live. With industry cooperation, they can adapt the Japanese concepts. This includes:

—Auditing

—Training

—Gathering Intelligence

—Quality Planning

—Increased Consulting

Establish Institutes For Quality Control And Productivity

Japan has demonstrated the importance of quality control and productivity. For America to give it competitive consideration we need means to keep top officials of industry and government and, particularly, our legislators informed, and provide means for broad support to their functions. Examples of needs that could be fulfilled are:

- Seminars by international experts to keep top officials of industry, government, and universities informed.

- Sponsor investigations of quality activities within America and in other nations. (The Quality Horizons Study by then Lt. Col. E.J. Westcott, sponsored by the Air Force Systems Command to investigate quality in Japan and leading European companies, is an example.)

- Sponsor research and development to improve quality systems and further ways to become more productive.

- Provide advanced education in company management for quality control and productivity.

- Provide advanced education to equip the quality control function to cope with high technology.

- Create model education programs centered on a quality control system which meets all the needs of a company. Avoid aggregation of miscellaneous, unconnected courses analogous to the offerings of a typical drug store.

- Maintain knowledge of the whereabouts of major, complex, expensive and unique equipment to test or measure quality.

* Provide a forum for interchange between industry and the university and a force for lobbying.

Such an institute to aid industry can only be created if it is supported by industry. A Board of Advisors from industry would be essential. Financial help may be needed initially though the institute should soon have the vitality to provide most of its own support.

Publishing

Fortune, Forbes and *Business Week* rarely provide articles by universities to industry on any subject. There is a need for such articles. The same applies for articles by industry officials to universities. The *Harvard Business Review* is unique. It is a bimonthly journal for professional managers and is a program in executive education of the Graduate School of Business Administration, Harvard University.

Professional societies such as ASQC provide excellent publications for professional quality control personnel. There is a similar need for quality control journals which address the needs of non-QC professionals, such as top industry and government officials, and managers who head functions that affect quality and productivity. A university-sponsored institute could publish the proposed journal and receive subscription and advertising fees to support it.

5. Utilizing Industry To Fulfill University Needs.

Below is a comprehensive list of ways corporations have supported universities, most including financial support. There is a great need for financial support as income from tuitions decreases with the passing of the baby boom. Federal funding has decreased. The negative impact on the public of the many reports cited earlier has resulted in fewer voluntary contributions from alumni and foundations. Continuation of these many supports will help universities to survive.

There are two areas worthy of emphasis. One is contracting to universities for basic education in quality control and productivity, and for increased involvement in the corporation's program. The other is to contract with universities for longer range and expanded roles described previously, such as providing university professors and instructors with longer range involvement at the company's plants. This increases their knowledge and experience, equipping them to improve their support to a company. The contract fee also aids the university.

Ways Corporations Have Helped Universities

At least three elements enter into corporate giving—*how* the money is given, *where* it is given to, and *for what purpose* it is given. These elements are not parallel: *how* may be restricted or unrestricted; *where* may be to a major university or a smaller liberal arts college, to a public or to a private institution, to a women's college, to a two-year or junior college or to a Negro institution; *for*

165

what purpose may be for a professorship, or it may be for library materials, interinstitutional cooperation, research, increased efficiency of operation, or a number of other purposes. A grant may go directly to an institution, or indirectly through an association or consortium of institutions. A grant may support one institution, or one discipline; it may be given for a demonstration or research project at one college which will benefit many other higher education institutions. Such a diversity of elements does not lend itself easily to classification.

It is the objective of the corporate section which follows to describe these disparate elements within corporate giving to higher education and to illustrate each with examples taken from programs of corporations and corporate-financed foundations. To do this, the Council for Financial Aid to Education has chosen to divide the material into three major categories—institutional aid; student aid; and employee- or company-related aid. Within the first category—institutional aid—the various elements given above are described and grant illustrations from corporate programs cited. Subheadings serve as guides to the material which follows in each case. Overlapping occurs, for not all grants within the subheadings, or even within the three major categories, fit perfectly. The major categories and subheadings are shown below.

PRODUCT QUALITY CONTROL SYSTEM MATRIX

TYPICAL QUALITY ACTIVITIES*	TYPICAL QUALITY EVENTS*	TYPICAL METHODS	TYPICAL PROCEDURES	TYPICALLY RESPONSIBLE	PHYSICAL RESOURCES
•Determine Customer Needs, Expectations**	-Review For Completeness	-Field Surveys -Bids -Proposals	-Customer Survey Procedure -Proposal Preparation Instructions	Marketing -Market Research Analyst -Sales Engineer	-Office Space/ Equipment -Computer
•Develop and Design Product •Evaluate Design Adequacy	-Multifunctional Design Review	-Mechanical/Electrical Layout -Prototype Evaluation -Lab Tests	-Product Evaluation Procedure and Checklist -Design Review Instructions	Engineering -Development Eng. -Design Eng. -Test Eng.	-Laboratory Space/ Eqp't. -Automated Drafting Equipment -Office Space/Eqp't. -Test Eqp't.
•Planning for Production -Materials -Facilities -People	-Multifunctional Review of Manufacturing Plan	-Order/Evaluate Materials -Order/Install Facilities/Equipment -Train People	-Purchased Material Evaluation Instructions -Equipment Control Procedures -Tool Control Procedures -Training Instructions	Manufacturing -Materials Specialist -Manufacturing Eng. -Mfg. Quality Assurance Eng. -Qual. Info. Eqp't. Eng. -Process Control Eng.	-Mfg. Plant -Machines -Tools -Office Space/Eqp't. -Computer -Laboratory Space/Eqp't.
•Manufacture Product	-Product Meeting Quality Requirements Available For Shipment	-Mechanical Assembly -Electrical Assembly -Automated Assembly -Chemical Processing	-Product Repair Procedures -Product Code Dating Instructions	Manufacturing -Direct Labor Operators	
•Assure Quality Of Manufactured Product	-Issuance Of Test And Inspection Plan	-Tests -Inspections -Audits -Analysis	-Test Instructions -Inspection Instructions -Audit Instructions -Analysis Procedures -Discrepant Material Control Procedure	Mfg. Quality Assurance -Mfg. Quality Assurance Eng. -Process Control Engineer -Qual. Info. Eqp't. Engineer	-Office Space/ Equipment -Computer -Laboratory Space/Eqp't. -Test Eqp't.
•Service Product	-Issuance Of Service Instructions	-Home Repairs -Service Shop Overhaul -Factory Repairs -Field Service	-Product Repair Procedures And Checklists -Product Test Procedures -Diagnostic Routines -Product Failure Reporting Procedures	Marketing -Service Technician -Mechanic -Electrician -Welder -Factory Personnel	-Space for Storage/ Repair -Special Tools And Test Eqp't. -Office Space/ Equipment -Special Communication Eqp't. (2-way radio, etc.)

*Note: Activity— a work
      —series of actions
      Event—important happening, important occurrence

**Note: Does not include consideration of price and delivery

Figure 14.1

CHAPTER 15
MUTUAL SUPPORT BETWEEN PROFESSIONAL SOCIETIES/ASSOCIATIONS AND INDUSTRY
GOOD SUPPORT BUT VITAL CHALLENGES

While mutual support is very good, professional societies/associations and industry face vital challenges that are key to America's ability to compete in quality and productivity. Despite the good support, America's reputation for quality and its productivity rates are the lowest among all the trade deficit nations. While American industry, particularly with the close help of ASQC, developed and applied a modern quality control discipline that has set the standard throughout the world, some mistakes were made. Union of Japanese Scientists and Engineers (JUSE) took advantage of our experience and applied initiative with their industries to correct the mistakes. In America these mistakes have been only partially corrected. There are many similarities but some major differences in the ways societies/associations and industry support each other in America and Japan. It is the differences that create more challenges. There is still much we can learn from each other. There is much less to be learned from the other trade deficit countries, as our situation is generally superior to theirs.

Some basic comparisons are needed before addressing the challenges. In America there are many professional societies/associations that provide support to industry for quality and productivity, while in Japan there are only a few. Some of the prominent American societies/associations include: ASQC, the Statistical Society of America, the National Industrial Conference Board, the National Security Industrial Association, the American Management Society, the Aerospace Industries Association, and the Quality Circles Institute. There are many more. In Japan, the most prominent professional society has been JUSE. A Japanese Society for Quality Control was established in 1971, oriented to the academic field. Other prominent organizations are the Japan Standards Association and Japan Management Association.

ASQC and JUSE are selected as the most prominent organizations to support industry in their respective countries. Both were founded at about the same time—1946 for ASQC and 1947 for JUSE. George Edwards, first president of ASQC, and Kenichi Koyanagi, the founder of JUSE, would be proud of the broad vision, acumen and vitality their organizations have applied to provide comprehensive and professional support to their industries. ASQC created an Education and Training Institute that provides short courses, seminars, home study courses and in-plant training programs. Through Quality Press and its extensive publications program, books and technical literature on the latest techniques and advancement in quality are offered. Other support is provided in the fields of standards, certifications, conventions and an employment registry.

In 1948, JUSE established within their framework the Quality Control Research Group, which has played an active role in quality control educational activities. The members are university professors of science and engineering and engineers from leading Japanese industrial firms. The group has continuously promoted quality control and provided a "linkage function" between statisticians—men of theory—and engineers—men of action—to constantly upgrade quality control practice in industry. JUSE and its Quality Control Research Group have close ties with industry and support from government agencies. They also provide technical literature and sponsor conventions.

Like America, there are a number of large companies and many small companies in Japan. In America, there are more of them. In America, industry supports professional societies by volunteering its employees to work on committees, usually paying the dues of its members and the costs of participating at seminars and conventions, subscribing to corporate membership, providing exhibits and using and paying for the services and literature offered. Japanese industry provides equivalent support. Because of geography, distances to be traveled are shorter and communication is easier in Japan.

With these comparisons in mind, let us now address the challenges.

TOP OFFICIAL LEADERSHIP AND INVOLVEMENT

As Japan acquired and adopted America's modern quality control system, the leaders of JUSE observed what they considered mistakes made by American industry. The most important, which we will deal with first, was the lack of leadership and involvement by the top officials of companies.

JUSE took the initiative in the early '50s to see that this did not occur in Japan. Ichiro Ishikawa, president of JUSE, initiated a succession of conferences with many top officials and managers of industry. JUSE also sponsored three visits by Dr. J.M. Juran. The first was in 1954. On each visit, Dr. Juran presented to top management of series of lectures on quality control, management, and how quality control is a vital part of management.

JUSE, with the assistance of Dr. Juran, successfully influenced the top officials. The result is that Japanese top managers do take personal leadership. They use the "president's audit" as a major tool. It is actually the president's annual quality plan and is described in Chapter 7 of this book.

Top officials receive education in quality control, directly participate in quality planning, and personally review company reports of quality performance. During Japan's annual "Quality Month," top officials attend the Top Management Quality Control Conference while staff and middle management attend their own quality control conference. During the year, top officials attend other conferences on quality control for top management. The top official personally leads the quality audit of his company. His top managers are part of the audit team.

The loss of America's international reputation for quality control began when top officials with expertise in other areas replaced those with expertise in manufacturing and quality control. Most of these new officials did not become educated in quality control because there were no readily available means to educate them. Some paid only lip service to quality control, but they did not lead or provide continuous involvement. Many approved and supported quality control, became good leaders, and remain competitive today. Any quality control manager will advise that the most important factor of a company's quality control effort is the leadership of its top official.

Many American top officials don't realize the effort required to turn around the competition in Japan. It had to do with how the Japanese have developed their discipline and how they are continuously improving it. Japan acquired extensive new knowledge and technology in quality control from many countries, though primarily from the United States. The Japanese digested this knowledge over time in such a way that it has succeeded in developing its own technology, building on the past knowledge and experience. Japan continues to capitalize on new knowledge in management and science, developed in Japan or abroad, to continuously improve its practice of quality control.

The onus is on top management of American industry. Most know what they must do, but they don't know how to do it. More importantly, they don't understand that quality control is a vital part of company management, nor what a top manager's quality control responsibilities are. They need to become more knowledgeable about quality control and about competitors' quality. They need a journal for top quality control management. *The challenge to professional societies and associations is to help top officials and top managers with these needs.* Dr. Deming, an Honorary Member of ASQC, has reached over 10,000 managers through seminars sponsored by The George Washington University. Dr. Juran, also an Honorary Member of ASQC, has lectured to thousands of top officials and top managers in America. The book you are now reading is published by ASQC. Chapter 7, "Top Management Involvement, Leadership, and Structure," tells managers how to provide leadership and continuing involvement. However, the need is greater than this. Other honorary members, past presidents and current presidents of professional societies/associations can help. So, too, can the officers and members associated with education and publications.

COMPANY-WIDE QUALITY CONTROL

JUSE observed a second mistake made in America and materially helped Japanese industry to avoid it. That mistake was to limit the control of quality, to an unsatisfactory degree, to one functional area of management (i.e., the quality control department). In Japan, quality control is a company treatment in which all people from top managers down to the rank and file, from the design and purchasing departments through manufacturing and sales, participate in a highly organized fashion. The Japanese system of new product development is integrated with and superimposed on that of quality control. JUSE had much to do with developing the Japanese concepts and educating and training all company personnel about the system and their responsibilities and functions in quality control.

In America in the '50s the newly developed disciplines emphasized organizations and the function of the quality control department. The problem was the need to upgrade leadership from the "inspection era" to a new powerful and comprehensive total quality control era. The typical organization of a quality control department would include quality systems engineering, quality control engineering, process control engineering, and supplier quality control and inspection. Functions for the quality control professionals in each organization were described in detail. The quality control manager's function was to manage the quality control department. He was accountable for quality. The quality operating procedures provided instructions primarily for quality control personnel. Where other organizations were involved in quality, their written instructions were included in their organization's publications. Usually there was no coordination between organizations for procedures and instructions. The originators of these disciplines recognized that, along with creating the world's best structure for assuring quality, they had oversold one-department control. Revised concepts appeared. The quality control manager was to be teacher and coordinator for the complete company quality control effort. Professional societies and companies developed quality control courses to educate and train personnel within the company outside of the quality control department. Many articles were written about the need for company-wide practice of quality control. But the facts are that most companies in America still retain most control and accountability for quality in a quality control department.

Again, most top officials have learned that they should change to company-wide quality control. The reason they don't is because they don't know how to do it. *The challenge to professional societies and associations is to continue and expand their activities to support a company-wide quality control system appropriate for America.* This includes continued development of model company-wide systems, new education for top officials and top management about such systems, and expansion of existing education and training activities for personnel who affect quality and are not in a quality control department.

MEETING THE NEEDS OF THE TOP, BOTTOM, AND OUTSIDE

There are similarities and differences in the way societies and associations support industry in America and in Japan. It is the differences that give each country opportunities to learn from each other. Japanese societies emphasize support to the top and the bottom and the outside while American societies emphasize the middle and the inside.

The Top

We have described JUSE's role in influencing top officials to provide leadership and involvement. Because of this JUSE had to follow up with means to educate and train the top officials. This required preparation of books, articles, and other educational material aimed at the role of quality control in company management and the top official's responsibilities for quality control. These needs were included in the above challenge for societies/associations because more help to top officials is needed to continuously improve the quality system. The orderly and continuous supply of intelligence of what foreign countries are doing to advance the management and sciences of quality control is needed. Reports based on a quick trip to Japan are innumerable but are not the answer. A better approach is more like the Quality Horizons study sponsored by the Air Force Systems Command. Considerable preparation and use of American Embassies were involved. Then extended visits were made to Japan and all major industrial countries of Europe and Great Britain. The arrangement to convey the knowledge to users involved many oral presentations and wide distribution of the written report. *The additional challenge for professional societies/associations is to sponsor similar surveys every two to three years.*

Still another challenge is the need for a linkage function between industry and government in the United States. There are committees appointed by professional societies for liaison with Congress, representatives on the various committees dealing with international trade, and other government officials involved with international trade. Professional societies/associations need to strengthen and expand these linkages.

The Bottom

The Quality Control Research Group of JUSE, consisting of university professors and engineers from industry, emphasizes attention to supervisors and their workers. They noted the intense interest of workers to study. The levels of education, including that of supervisors and workers, are high in industry. JUSE discovered that most technical publications about quality control, and particularly statistics, were too academically oriented and overly technical to be useful to supervisors and their employees. In response, JUSE prepared education and training courses, seminars, and other literature for exclusive use of supervisors and workers. This included preparation of *Guide to Quality Control*, which teaches analytical and statistical methods by Dr. Kaoru Ishikawa, a professor at Tokyo University.

The concept of quality circles was created as a means to make more effective use of supervisors in 1961 by the editors of the magazine *Quality Control*, published by JUSE. They sponsored a symposium on "Some Problems Facing the Shop Foreman." The result was a new journal, *QC for Foremen*. It was priced to be affordable by all foremen and not only provided articles for foremen but encouraged articles written by them. In addition, quality circles were established for the foreman and his workers. (It's interesting to inject that zero defects was established at around

173

the same time in 1962 in the United States. JUSE maintains the national head-quarters for quality circles.) All circles are registered with headquarters. In addition to creating quality circles, development of conventions followed whereby foremen and their workers share knowledge learned in quality circles. *The challenge to professional societies/associations is to increase their attention to developing education and training for supervisors and hourly workers, and increase attention to providing guidance on adaptation of quality circles to American workers.*

The Outside

As previously discussed, the Japanese emphasize the outside (i.e., company-wide practice of quality control), while we, often inadvertently, emphasize the inside (i.e., quality control in one department). *Again, the challenge to professional societies/associations is to aid industry to change from inside to outside.*

PRODUCTIVITY

There is a final challenge to professional societies/associations, but there are no easy handles to grab on to. It has to do with "productivity." There is no lack of interest by top officials of industry in productivity. Also, there is no lack of literature about productivity. The ways by which productivity is being improved are innumerable. Still, American rates of productivity increase are continually lower than the trade deficit countries. We need some fundamental definitions, principles and practices, and better organization of education and training material for productivity. Productivity is not quite a discipline. At the international and national level there are definitions for, and measurement of, productivity. At the individual worker level, whose output is number of items, it is easy to define productivity. But managers are faced with the need to define and measure productivity at various places within the company. They need guidance. In 1985, Peter Drucker wrote *Innovation and Entrepreneurship.* There is also a need for "innovation and productivity." Quality control and productivity are closely associated, but few people understand the relationship. We need education. Though productivity is not a discipline it needs some principles and practices about how to achieve and improve it. *The challenge to professional societies/associations is to institute a long-range program to contribute to these needs.*

CHAPTER 16
COMMUNICATION AND REWARDS
THE NEEDS

There is a need for powerful and creditable ways to communicate with and motivate employees and suppliers to sustain the quality effort. Also we need a system of rewards for extraordinary efforts.

This chapter selects already successful methods and new methods to communicate developed in America and Japan. It identifies methods that should be discarded or avoided and recommends awards that both recognize accomplishment and increase the level of interest in and awareness of the importance of quality control and productivity.

SOURCES FOR POWERFUL COMMUNICATION — METHODS AND REWARDS

In the history of American industry, there have been several times when managers needed to motivate employees to improve quality and productivity and to provide rewards.

One occasion was in the '50s, when America progressed from the "inspection era" to use of the modern quality control discipline. Another occurred as "zero defects" and other motivation programs swept across the United States during the '60s. There have been times when corporations, as well as the military services, observed a falling off in their levels of quality and initiated "quality improvement programs."

More recently, the competition with Japan has stimulated several of our progressive companies to develop highly effective ways for upper management to reach their employees and to reward them. As top officials in Japan led their industrial revolution, they developed ways to communicate with and influence employees and to reward them. The means for communication and reward described in this chapter were selected from these experiences and the new American and Japanese developments.

Initial Communication With Employees

When creditable progress has been made in removing obstacles and improving the environment it is time to begin more effective means for using all employees to improve products, services and systems. The top official should introduce this phase to all employees in a meeting. Before the meeting takes place it is most

175

useful to have the latest iteration of the company philosophy and balanced objectives that benefit both the company and employees. The plans for rewards must also be completed. Most important, the purposes of the meeting must be clear:

- To inform employees of the nature of the foreign competition and that it is a long-term, continuous concern. To convey the importance of quality and productivity in the competition. To emphasize the need for employees' involvement, to improve quality and productivity of products, services and systems.

- To create a positive impression of the leadership of the top official and his top managers, and management's intent to share fairly any benefits obtained from the added effort of employees.

- To make employees feel challenged and want to increase their involvement on the team that will overcome the competition. To make the employees feel proud of being part of a company that wants to increase its standards.

A good way to announce the meeting is by a letter from the top official to each employee and his family sent to the employee's home address.

The atmosphere of the meeting should be positive, friendly, and inspire trust and confidence. The top official and his top managers should be on the stage. It is desirable to have a top official from a customer present as well. Showmanship in good taste helps but hoopla is to be avoided. The top officials should give the primary messages and some other top managers should give supporting presentations. A talk from a customer official adds a great deal.

Aim the presentations to meet the purposes of the meeting. It is the appropriate place to convey the new company philosophy and the associated company objectives, balanced to benefit both company and employees. It is an opportunity for top management to show empathy for any past obstacles or unsatisfactory environments and describe the continuing efforts of management to remove them and improve the environment.

Describe the top management structure, showing its leadership and involvement through the functions of the steering arm, the incentives and resources team, the Customer Ombudsman and the president's plan. Ways for more effective employee involvement can be described, including participation on diagnostic teams, management quality circles, supervisor and hourly employee quality circles and value engineering teams.

Describe the company's initiative to benefit the individual employees while improving their effectiveness. This includes revitalizing the company-sponsored education and training program, encouraging participation of managers in professional societies, creating new attention to improving the talents of supervisors and hourly workers, improving the company libraries, and providing experimental laboratories and shops. The incentives and resources team should explain the plans for rewards that may range from recognitions to profit sharing. As open communication builds trust, it would be appropriate to announce semi-annual or annual top-management reports of the business for all employees.

The planning and preparations for this meeting should learn from and avoid the negative experiences with "kick-off" meetings as practiced with zero defects and similar motivation programs. Excess hoopla resulted in loss of credibility and demotivation of employees. The excess hoopla involved wheelbarrows full of pledge cards signed by all employees, the "teaser" campaign, the use of bands, the application of pep rally tactics sometimes led by an official rally chairman. A little showmanship in good taste should substitute for hoopla. The good features of these meetings were the leadership of the top official, the involvement of his top managers and the presence of customers.

Initial Communications With Suppliers

The word will spread rapidly to suppliers about the meeting with employees. They will relate it to what they see on television and read every day in the papers and news journals. Many have lost business to foreign suppliers. They are conditioned to a need for change but lack a forum for making change. The forum must be the company and its suppliers working together. An initial meeting with regular suppliers is in order.

Preparation for the supplier meeting should include the latest iteration of the company philosophy and policies related to suppliers. Plans should be in hand to change adversarial relations within the company and remove other obstacles to permit more effective relationships with suppliers. Goals for improved relations between company and supplier should be prepared, as well as a framework of rewards to suppliers.

The purposes of the meeting are:

- To inform suppliers of the nature of the competition; that it is a long-term, continuing concern; and of the importance of quality and productivity in the competition.

- To inform suppliers of the relationship between companies and suppliers in Japan that has been a key to achieving superior quality at lower costs.

- To provide goals for more effective relations between the company and its suppliers and to address the benefits.

- To create a positive impression for the top official and teamwork between his top managers responsible for purchasing and quality control.

- To make suppliers feel challenged, to make them want to provide more effective involvement and be part of a team that will overcome the competition. To make supplier officials proud of the intent to raise standards and provide higher quality products and services.

Better Communications To Sustain Motivation Of
Employees And Suppliers

The initial communications to all employees and the most active suppliers have occurred. The scenario continues with the need for ways to communicate that will sustain, for an infinite period, the effective involvement of all employees. Many companies retain outmoded means of communication to sustain employee interest in quality control and productivity. These methods have not been effective in motivating employees and should be discarded or corrected. Examples are:

- *Use of posters.* Employees know the company contracts with a supplier who provides suitable frames for installation in locations around the plant. Each month the supplier sends a new set of posters. They no longer motivate if they ever did.

- *Infrequent visits to work areas.* Most officials and top managers are so busy they seldom visit the work areas and talk with employees. When they do it's usually to accompany a customer tour, a quick tour to show presence, or to witness a major problem that has occurred.

- *Communication via channels.* Upper management communicates with middle management who communicates with front-line management who transmits to the supervisor who communicates with the operator. If it's a word of appreciation, the effect is watered down. If it's a problem, the operator probably already knows about it. If it's a request for information, it's a rare opportunity to become involved and the employee enthusiastically passes the information back up through channels.

Better ways to achieve communication are:

- *Getting managers to where the work is.* Hewlett-Packard calls it MBWA— "Management by Wandering Around." United Airlines calls it "Visible Management." Top managers in these corporations have broken from tradition. The normal day-in and day-out practice is for top managers to roam the work areas asking questions, discussing ideas, and encouraging innovation and improvements.

- *Locating the manager where the work is.* Texas Instruments initiated this practice 20 years ago. It greatly increases communication with the people who do the work.

- *Locating in adjoining offices managers of functions that are natural adversaries.* Quality control managers and production managers along with purchasing managers and supplier quality control managers are examples. This closeness insures communication and better understanding of each other's problems leading to improved teamwork.

- *The open door policy.* An old concept but one that has been perfected by such corporations as IBM and Delta Airlines.

178

- *Diagnostic teams, quality circles and value engineering teams.* These are major contributors for communication across organizational lines which is vitally needed in traditional organizations. While each group provides a way for free flow of communication within the group it also provides an opportunity for communication with middle and upper management. Middle and upper management presence in the audience that receives oral reports from these groups provides the opportunity for questions and exchange of ideas.

- *The president's audit.* In Japan, normal practice is for the company president to lead a quality control audit at periodic intervals. He is accompanied by his top managers and university consultants. It involves visits to work areas and communication and exchange of information between the top official and top management and employees of all echelons and categories.

- *The president's plan.* This provides written communications approved by the president and his steering arm and is directed to the many working groups who supplied recommendations and will implement the work.

- *Monthly letters prepared by customers or the top official or a top manager to replace posters.* There are personal communications about needs for attention, recognition of accomplishment, and business news that are updated monthly and posted in work areas. They are good replacements for posters.

- *Use of the media.* Employees and their families feel great pride when the media expresses esteem for the company. Favorable correspondence from customers, federal, state and local governments and other sources that are printed in the local press or appear on television are sure motivations of pride.

- *Use of the house organ.* A mundane house organ can be revitalized by a regular column from the top official who may rotate with other top managers. A special quality and productivity column can be added as well.

Additional opportunities to improve communication may occur upon special occasions such as National Quality Month, Annual Vendor Day, or during national conferences.

Special Occasions

National Quality Month

Japan established November as its National Quality Month in 1960. It is celebrated in industry, government and professional associations across the country. Highlights are the conferences that occur during that month and include:

—Top Management Quality Control Conference

—Staff and Middle Management Quality Control Conferences

—Foreman Quality Control Conferences

—Consumer Quality Control Conferences

In 1984, a U.S. Congressional Resolution and a Presidential Proclamation established October as America's National Quality Month. For the first five years ASQC will be in the forefront of this annual October event. It will be featured in their publications. This is an outstanding opportunity for industry, the government and universities to acquaint employees and suppliers with their commitments to continued improvements in quality of products and services.

Annual Vendor Day

Several companies and divisions of large American corporations sponsor an Annual Vendor Day. It is an outstanding opportunity to communicate to suppliers the importance of quality control and productivity in the competition with foreign countries. It is an opportunity to increase and strengthen suppliers' commitment and involvement in improving the quality and productivity of their products and services. A primary purpose is to communicate the company's appreciation of extraordinary achievements for quality and productivity during the past year by the presentation of awards to the suppliers.

National Conferences

ASQC Annual Quality Congress

The Annual Quality Congress of the American Society for Quality Control is the nation's oldest and the world's most comprehensive and largest technical conference devoted to quality. The ASQC Board that plans and manages conferences draws on 13 Divisions representing different industries and functions, 11 Technical Committees, 197 Sections across America and in foreign countries, and 435 corporate members in the United States and 61 foreign countries. It is a single source from which any company can learn the latest advancements in the management and science of quality control and thereby continuously improve its quality system.

NSIA Semi-Annual Conferences

The National Security Industrial Association, often with the Aerospace Industries Association, sponsors semi-annual conferences devoted to quality control within the military-industrial complex. It acts as a liaison and has close relations with the top quality control officials in the office of the Secretary of Defense and each military service. Any company engaged in weapons acquisition should belong as it is a single source of information about new military requirements and studies of potential new requirements.

A Japanese Conference For Foremen

In Japan, the application of quality circles has led to major conferences for foremen. They provide opportunities for foremen and key workers who have made a significant contribution within a quality circle to present a paper about it for use by other foremen and workers. As more attention is given to the education and training of supervisors in America and better adaptation of quality circles occurs, we may develop some type of local and regional conferences for supervisors.

REWARDS

The need for creditable and powerful means of communication is complemented by the need for rewards that assist management in motivating more effective use of people. Except for the distinguished awards provided by the American Society for Quality Control, there is a notable absence of important, well-known American awards exclusively for quality control, for either companies or individuals. Another exception is the NASA Excellence Award for Quality and Productivity administered by ASQC. The Japanese do have distinguished awards exclusively for quality control for companies and individuals.

Awards—A Means to Motivate or to Demotivate

This book describes an incentives and resources team composed of upper managers on the staff of the top official, which reports to him. The right award presented for the right purpose not only gives recognition and reward to the recipient, but makes all employees aware of the importance of quality control and productivity and motivates continued effort.

The wrong award presented for the wrong reason undermines the credibility of management and results in demotivation of employees. There are many unfair practices that result in some recipient receiving larger awards than their contribution warrants, and others whose awards are less than their contribution warrants. This seriously impairs management's reputation for fairness. Examples of negative awards which should be avoided are:

Prolific Awards—Awards that are initially coveted but become so prolific they become meaningless and eventually cause demotivation. An example is: the framed "zero defects" certificates and certificates for similar prolific issues which cover the walls by the desks of nearly all employees.

Wrong Awards—Awards or formal certificates for little or no effort or attainment, issued as much as an advertisement for the originator as for the benefit of the receiver. The lobbies of most companies in America are full of them, and hundreds of lobbies contain the same award.

Unfair Awards—Money, stock and many kinds of perks awarded executives for their extra contribution to the business, but little or no award to those other employees whose extra contribution also helped earn the awards.

Unsatisfactory Use of Good Awards—Instead of using the award to promote competition and motivate employees, it receives little attention until time to present it rolls around. Then it's a scramble to locate qualified recipients.

Insufficient Awards for Suppliers—Awards are a major opportunity to motivate suppliers. There is a paucity of such awards.

Awards for the Wrong Reason—A competent awards board will assure that the purpose for an award is clear and thoroughly promulgated and that there are specific criteria or guides for qualifying. It will carefully screen candidates to ensure each meets the criteria.

When there is no board, an incompetent board, or a biased board, rewards for the wrong reason often occur. Wrong reasons for rewards are too numerous to list but include:

—It's the other person's turn for an award.

—The dynamic charisma along with the amount of dust stirred up must warrant an award.

—We all know this person—a close friend or business associate.

—He did something else good a month ago and didn't get a reward.

The Most Effective Rewards

The rewards that have been and still are most effective in inspiring companies and individuals are characterized by:

- Requirements for exceeding high standards of performance.
- Concern with long-term sustained high levels of performance.
- Competition between excellent companies or individuals.
- Only one recipient or a very few recipients at a time.
- Competent boards or authorities who actually evaluate performance.
- The award is widely recognized and respected.
- Attainment provides long-term benefits to a company's business or an individual's career.

American And Japanese Examples Of Awards For Companies

The awards described below comply reasonably with the characteristics described above for "Most Effective Awards," with some qualifications as noted. All of the Japanese awards are oriented to quality and productivity. Quality and productivity are major factors in the American awards.

The U.S Navy Department's "E" for Excellence Award is the oldest award. It was originated before World War II to motivate economy of operations at all ships and stations. During the war it was applied to industry and still exists. Its high standards also apply to quality and productivity. They are verified by teams who conduct surveys at candidate companies. The "E" for Excellence flag over the company's building is an inspiration to all employees.

The Defense Department promoted the zero defects program. It created the Participation, Achievement, Craftsmanship and Sustained Craftsmanship Awards for companies. This program is now discontinued. Despite the hoopla and exaggerated measurements, the programs spread through industry, educational institutions, hospitals and banks. Post evaluations by the Air Force indicated substantially improved quality and productivity. Initially the awards were highly coveted, but their proliferation reduced their value. It is noteworthy that the Department of Defense only provided awards to the defense industry. Despite lack of rewards, the program spread to civilian industry and innumerable types of other institutions.

The most effective award for companies in Japan is the Deming Application Prize. JUSE instituted the prize. It is named in honor of W. Edwards Deming for his contribution to the improvement of Japan's economy. The award is presented to a company that has excelled in at least seven of the ten quality criteria established by JUSE.

There is also a Japanese "Q" for Quality Award, which is somewhat similar to the U.S. Navy's "E" for Excellence Award, but is exclusively for quality. The "Q" for Quality flags are apparent flying over the buildings of Japanese companies. The Minister of International Trade and Industry in Japan also provides a prize for standardization.

Awards For Quality By ASQC

The awards listed below are sponsored by the American Society for Quality Control. All pertain to quality. ASQC has impressive boards for each award. Each award fully complies with the characteristics for "Most Effective Awards." The awards are:

—Brumbaugh Award

—Edwards Medal

—E.L. Grant Award

—Shewhart Medal

—E.J. Lancaster Award

NSIA Awards

The NSIA has an awards board that provides awards in which quality and productivity are factors. The NSIA also has "Certificates of Recognition." The certificates are for major contributions while serving on NSIA committees in support of the Defense Department. There are many types of contributions, of which quality is one, for extraordinary effort over an extended period of time. A letter of appreciation to the person's company transmits the certificate, and press releases are sent to local news media. The award is signed by the NSIA president or a flag officer of the military services.

Corporation Awards to Employees

Practically all corporations have awards for high standards. Quality is sometimes a factor, but awards exclusively for quality are infrequent. The reward that is becoming more commonplace is profit sharing. The plans range widely. One type assigns a set percentage of profit for employees and each receives an amount that never changes. In another, the share of profits is incorporated into incentive programs.

Supplier Awards

Some corporations establish awards for suppliers. When I was associated with the General Electric Company, awards used by one division that were particularly effective were:

- *Monthly Vendor Award.* The award was made to a single vendor who made the greatest contribution during the month and who consistently supplied products or services of above satisfactory quality. Purchasing agents, quality control engineers, design engineers and production engineers were asked to submit nominations each month with a written report of the contribution. The vendors' performance ratings were always reviewed. Visits to vendors' businesses were made for verification when necessary. The final decision was made based on a review conducted by the quality control department manager, the manufacturing department manager, and the employee relations manager. The award would be presented by all three department heads to the top vendor official at a ceremony at the vendor's premises witnessed by all employees. A letter from a vice president of General Electric Company accompanied the award and was read at the ceremony. The chief of the regional small business administration was invariably in attendance.

- *Vendor of the Year Award.* The division honored its suppliers by sponsoring an Annual Vendor Day. The announcement invited all active vendors and their employees to visit the plant, where they were given tours. They were also shown exhibits of company products assembled from the components supplied by the vendors. After a dinner given for the top vendor officials, an award ceremony was conducted. The vendor of the year was chosen by the same process as the vendor of the month. The division vice president presented the award, and in attendance would be the division's purchasing, quality control, and production managers, and state and city officials. Members of the press would be there as well and press releases would be supplied to them.

BIBLIOGRAPHY

JAPANESE AND OTHER INTERNATIONAL REFERENCES

Dreyfack, R. *Making It In Management the Japanese Way.* Rockville Center, N.Y.: Farnsworth Publishing Co., 1982.

Ishikawa, K. *Guide to Quality Control.* Tokyo: Asian Productivity Organization, 1972.

Ishikawa. "Quality Control in Japan." *Reports of QC Circle Activities,* No. 1. Tokyo: JUSE, 1968.

Ishikawa. "Quality Control System in Japan." *Reports of QC Circle Activities,* No. 6. Tokyo: JUSE, 1973.

Gregg, N. T. "Hagi: Where Japan's Revolution Began." *National Geographic:* June 1984, pp. 751-772.

Grove, N. "Taiwan." *National Geographic:* January 1982, pp. 92-119.

Koyanagi, K. *The Deming Prize.* Tokyo: JUSE, 1960.

Niland, P. *Quality Circles.* Tokyo: McGraw-Hill in collaboration with Asian Productivity Organization, 1971.

Ohba, K. "Present Status of QC Circle Activities in Japan." *Reports of QC Circle Activities,* No. 6. Tokyo: JUSE, 1973.

Ouchi, W. G. *Theory Z.* Philippines: Addison-Wesley, 1981.

Pascale, R. T. and A. G. Athos. *The Art of Japanese Management.* New York: Warner Books, 1982.

Phillips, K. P. "America Must Look Out for Number One." *Washington Post,* 16 December 1984.

Richmond, F. and M. L. Kahan. *How to Beat the Japanese at Their Own Game.* Englewood Cliffs, N.J.: Prentice Hall, 1983.

AMERICAN REFERENCES

"America's Competitive Challenge: The Need for a National Response." *Report of the Business-Higher Education Forum to the President of the United States.* By Business-Higher Education Forum. Washington, D.C.: Government Printing Office [exact date unknown].

Bowles, S. and H. Gintis. *Schooling in Capitalistic America.* New York: Harper & Row, 1976.

Deming, W. E. *Quality, Productivity and Competitive Position.* Cambridge: Massachusetts Institute of Technology, 1982.

DeWar, D. L. *Quality Circles Leader Manual and Instructional Guide.* Red Bluff, Calif.: Quality Circle Inst., 1980.

DeWar. *Quality Circles Member Manual.* Red Bluff, Calif.: Quality Circle Inst., 1980.

Drucker, P. F. *Innovation and Entrepreneurship: Practice and Principles.* New York: Harper & Row, 1985.

Feigenbaum, A. V. *Total Quality Control,* 3rd edition. New York: McGraw-Hill, 1983.

Hughes, C. L. *Goal Setting: Key to Individual and Organizational Effectiveness.* New York: American Management Assoc., 1965.

Halpin, J. F. *Zero Defects*. New York: McGraw-Hill, 1966.

Leavitt, H. J. *Managerial Psychology*, 2nd edition. Chicago: Univ. of Chicago Press, 1964.

Juran, J. M. "Consumerism and Product Quality." *Quality Progress*, Vol. 3, No. 7, July 1970, pp. 18-27.

Juran. *Managerial Breakthrough*. New York: McGraw-Hill, 1964.

Juran. "Mobilizing for the 1970's." *Quality Progress*, Vol. 2, No. 8, August 1969, pp. 8-17.

Juran. *Quality Control Handbook*, 3rd edition. New York: McGraw-Hill, 1974.

Juran and F. M. Gryna, Jr. *Quality Planning and Analysis*. New York: McGraw-Hill, 1970.

Lawler, E. E., III and S. A. Mohrman. "Quality Circles After the Fad." *Harvard Business Review*, Vol. 63, No. 1, 1985, pp. 64-71.

Mann, N. R. *The Keys to Excellence*. Los Angeles: Prestwick Books, 1985.

Miles, L. D. *Techniques of Value Analysis and Engineering*, 2nd edition. New York: McGraw-Hill, 1972.

"A Nation at Risk." *Report on the National Commission on Excellence in Education*. By T. H. Bell, Secretary of Education. Washington, D.C.: Government Printing Office, 1983.

Office of the Assistant Secretary of Defense (Installation and Logistics). *A Guide to Zero Defects: Quality and Reliability Assurance Handbook*, No. 4115.12H. Washington, D.C.: Government Printing Office, 1965.

Parker, G. T. *The Writing on the Wall*. New York: Simon & Schuster, 1979.

Peters, T. J. and N. Austin. *A Passion for Excellence*. New York: Random House, 1985.

Peters and R. H. Waterman, Jr. *In Search of Excellence*. New York: Harper & Row, 1984.

Richards, M. D. and P. S. Greenlaw. *Management Decisions and Behavior*. Homewood, Ill.: Richard D. Irwin, Inc., 1972.

Schock, J. E., Jr. "Quality Motivation as a Management Concept." Paper presented at the 21st Annual Technical Conference of the American Society for Quality Control, Chicago, 31 May 1967.

CONCEPTS AND PRINCIPLES FOR INVOLVING PEOPLE EFFECTIVELY

Argyris, C. *Integrating the Individual and the Organization*. New York: John Wiley & Sons, 1964.

Argyris. *Interpersonal Competence and Organization Effectiveness*. Homewood, Ill.: Irwin-Dorsey, 1962.

Argyris. *Personality and Organization*. New York: Harper, 1957.

Batten, J. D. *Tough-Minded Management*. New York: American Management Assoc., 1963.

Blake, R. and J. S. Mouton. *The Managerial Grid*. Houston: Gulf Publishing, 1964.

Chaney, F. B. "Personnel Training and Evaluation for Quality Motivation." *Quality Motivation Workbook*. Milwaukee, Wis.: ASQC, 1978, pp. 91-106.

Delana, D. D. "A Steelworker Talks Motivation." *Industry Week*, 14 January 1974, pp. 26-30.

Gardner, J. W. *Excellence*. New York: Harper & Row, 1961.

Gardner. *Self-Renewal: The Individual and the Innovative Society*. New York: Harper & Row, 1963.

Gellerman, S. W. *Motivation and Productivity*. New York: American Management Assoc., 1963.

Herzberg, F. "The New Industrial Psychology." *Industrial and Labor Relations Review*, April 1965, pp. 364-376.

Herzberg. *Work and the Nature of Man*. Cleveland: World Publishing, 1966.

Johnson, R. G. *The Appraisal Interview Guide*. New York: AMACOM, 1979.

Likert, R. *The Human Organization*. New York: McGraw-Hill, 1967.

Likert. *New Patterns of Management*. New York: McGraw-Hill, 1961.

Maslow, A. H. *Eupsychian Management*. Homewood, Ill.: Irwin-Dorsey, 1965.

Maslow. *Toward a Psychology of Being*. New York: VanNostrand Co., 1968.

Mayo, E. *Human Problems of an Industrial Civilization*. Cambridge: Harvard Univ. Press, 1933.

McGregor, D. *The Human Side of Enterprise*. New York: McGraw-Hill, 1960.

McGregor. *Leadership and Motivation*. Cambridge: Massachusetts Institute of Technology, 1966.

McGregor. *The Professional Manager*. New York: McGraw-Hill, 1967.

Myers, M. S. "Who Are Your Motivated Workers?" *Harvard Business Review*, January/February 1965.

Pierce, R. J. "Current and Advanced Motivational Methods Utilized in Zero Defects Programs." Paper presented to U.S. Air Force Zero Defects Council, Randolph AFB, San Antonio: 16 March 1967.

Pierce. "Education for Excellence: The Development of Technical Project Engineers." *Journal of Environmental Sciences*, Vol. 8, No. 1, February 1965, pp. 12-18.

Pierce. "Future of Motivation Programs." *The Logistics Review and Military Logistics Journal*, Vol. 2, No. 9, 1966, pp. 5-7.

Pierce. "Future of Quality Motivation as a Recognized Management Tool." Paper presented at 9th Annual Symposium on Quality Control Methods and Management, Villanova Univ., 13 November 1965.

Pierce and S. C. Streep. "Successful Motivation Programs." *Industrial Quality Control*, Vol. 22, No. 12, June 1966, pp. 654-658.

Pierce, F. B. Chaney, E. W. Ellis, P. D. Metzler, J. A. Russell, H. E. Schock, L. P. Sinotte and H. M. Weiss. *Quality Motivation Workbook*. Milwaukee, Wis.: ASQC, 1978.

Regis, W. H. *Study on Human Factors Related to Quality and Reliability of Unmanned Spacecraft Components*. Washington, D.C.: George Washington Univ. (Center for the Behavioral Sciences), March 1965.

Rush, H. M. F. *Behavioral Science Concepts and Management Applications* (Conference Board Report, No. SRP 216). New York: National Industrial Conference Board, 1969.

" 'Something is Out of Whack' in U.S. Business Management," a conversation with Tom Peters. *U.S. News & World Report*, 15 July 1985, pp. 53-54.

Weiss, H. M. "Quality Motivation: Long-Range Management Tool." Paper presented at 10th Annual Symposium on Quality Control Methods and Management, Villanova Univ., 12 November 1966.